PEACOCK
COLORING BOOK

Get FREE printable coloring pages and discounted book prices sent straight to your e-mail inbox every week!

Sign up at:

www.adultcoloringworld.net

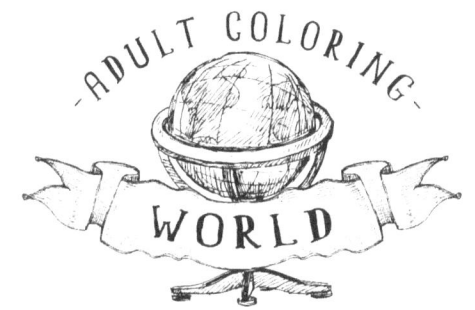

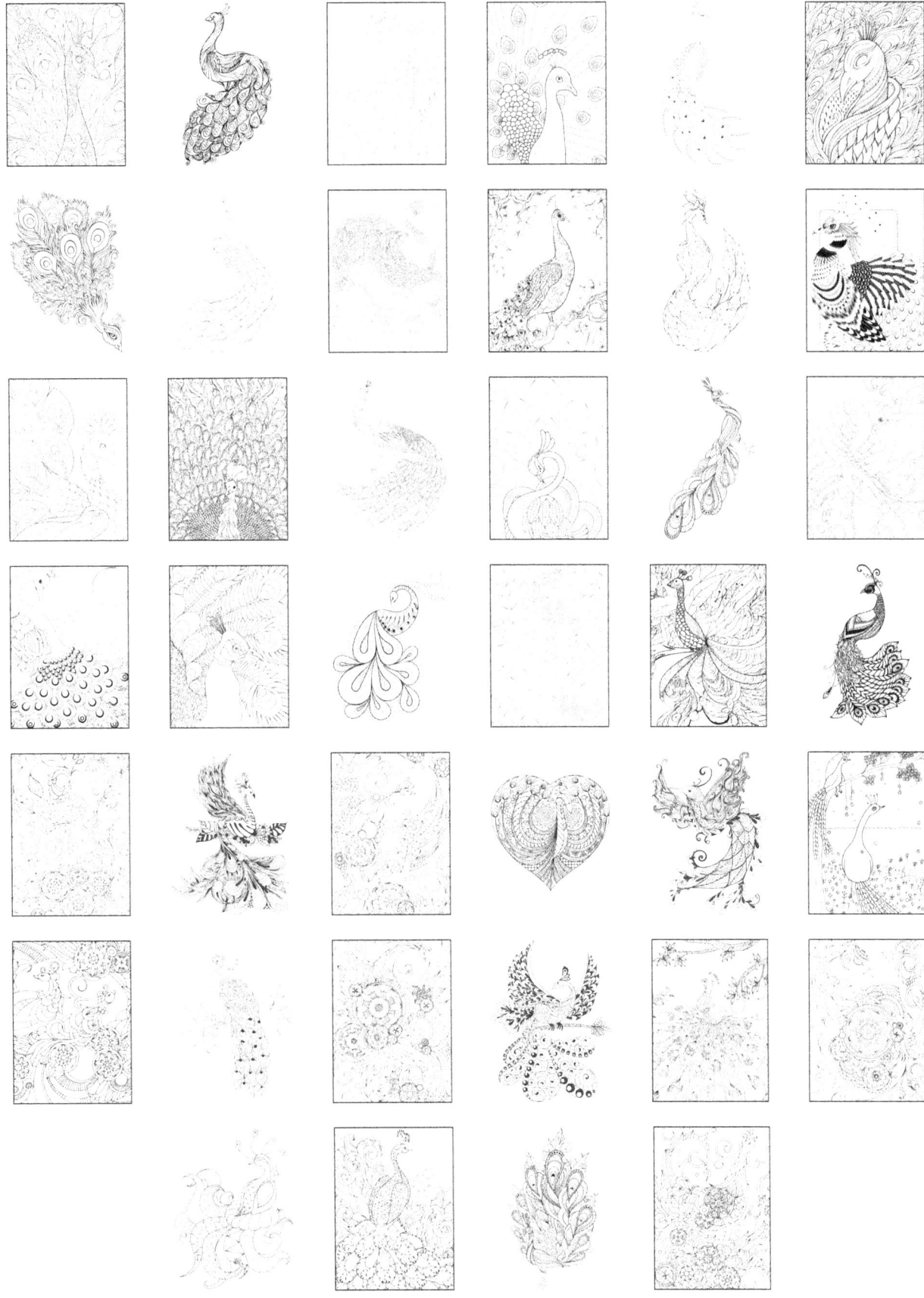

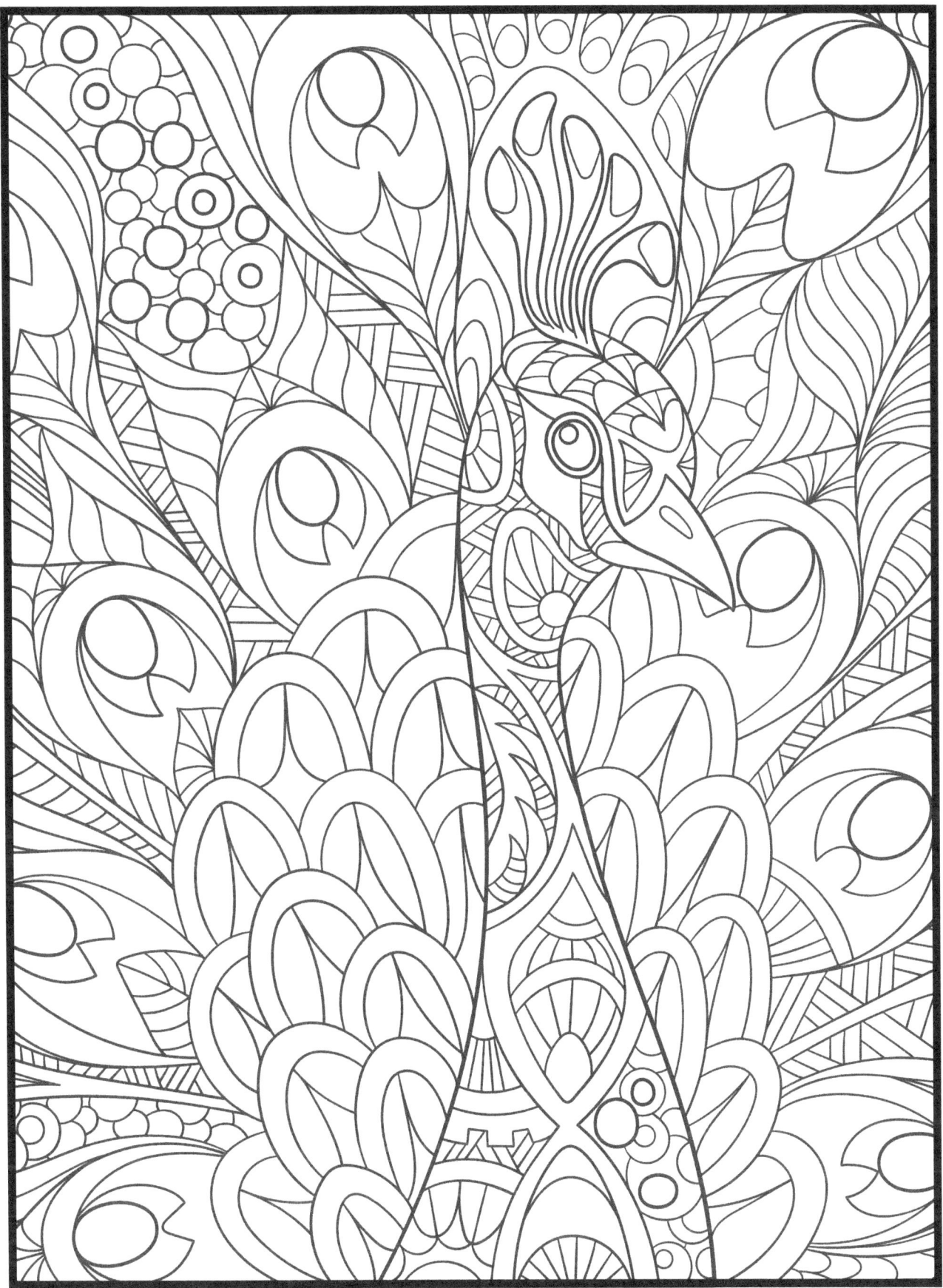

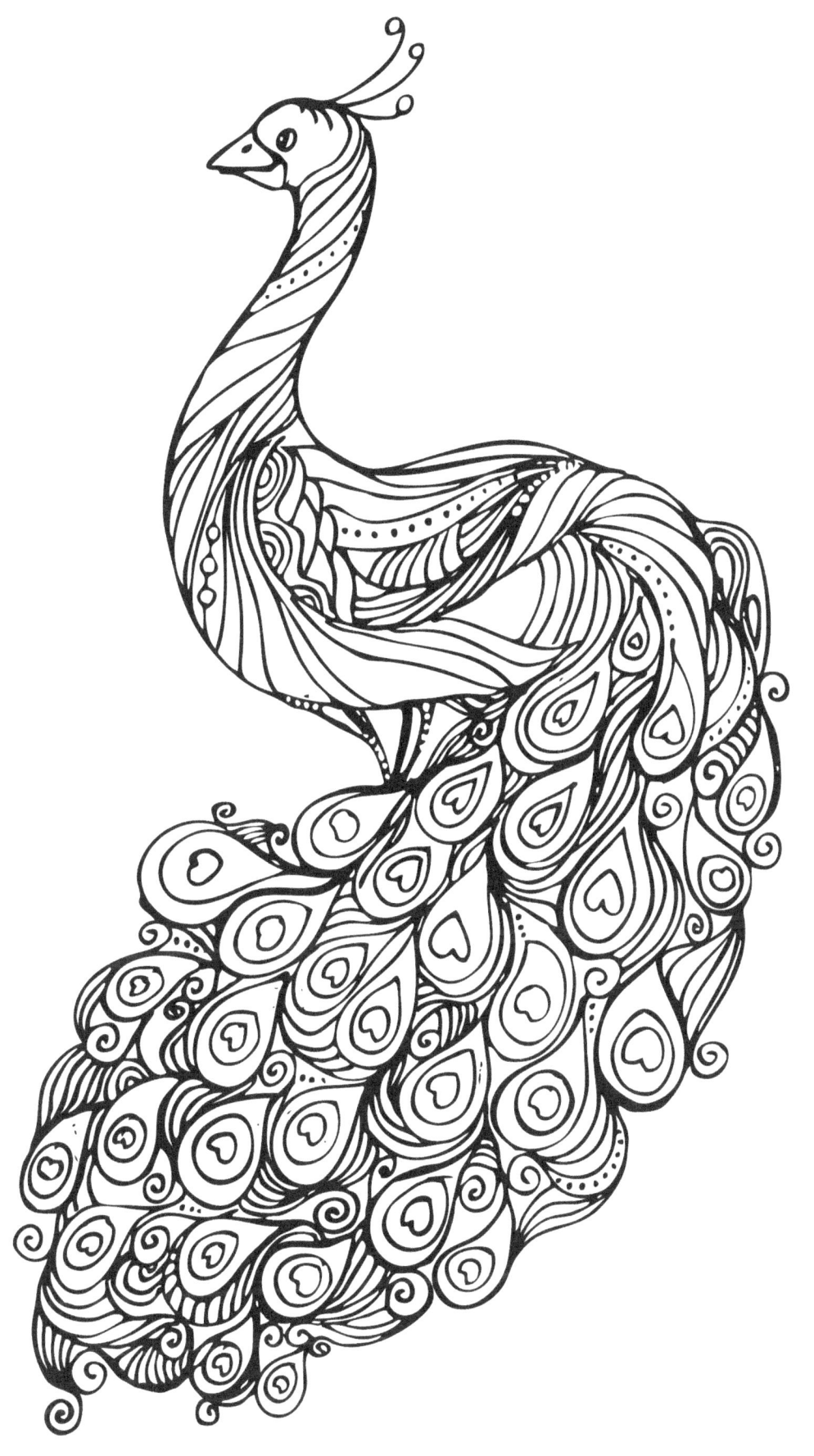

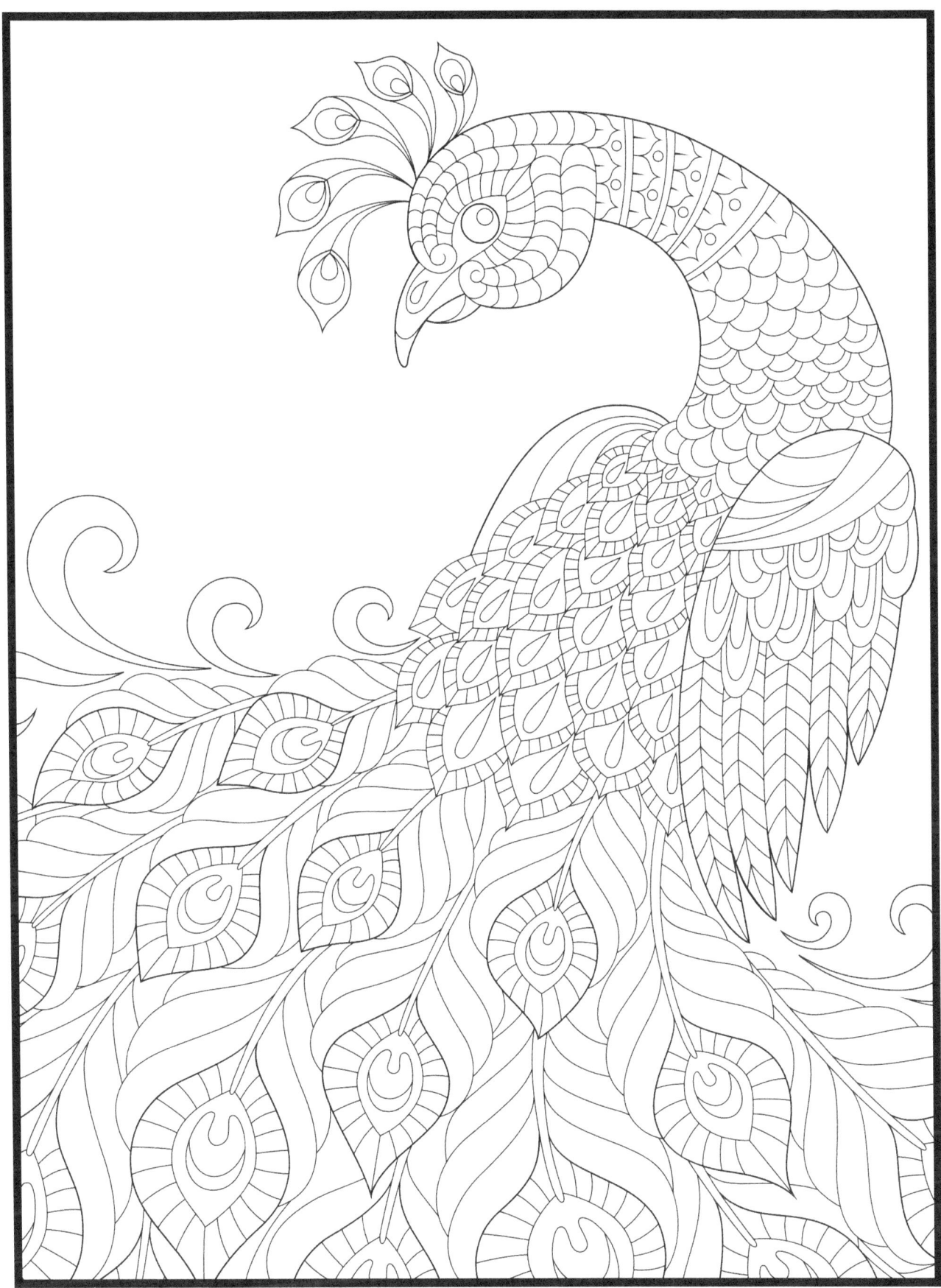

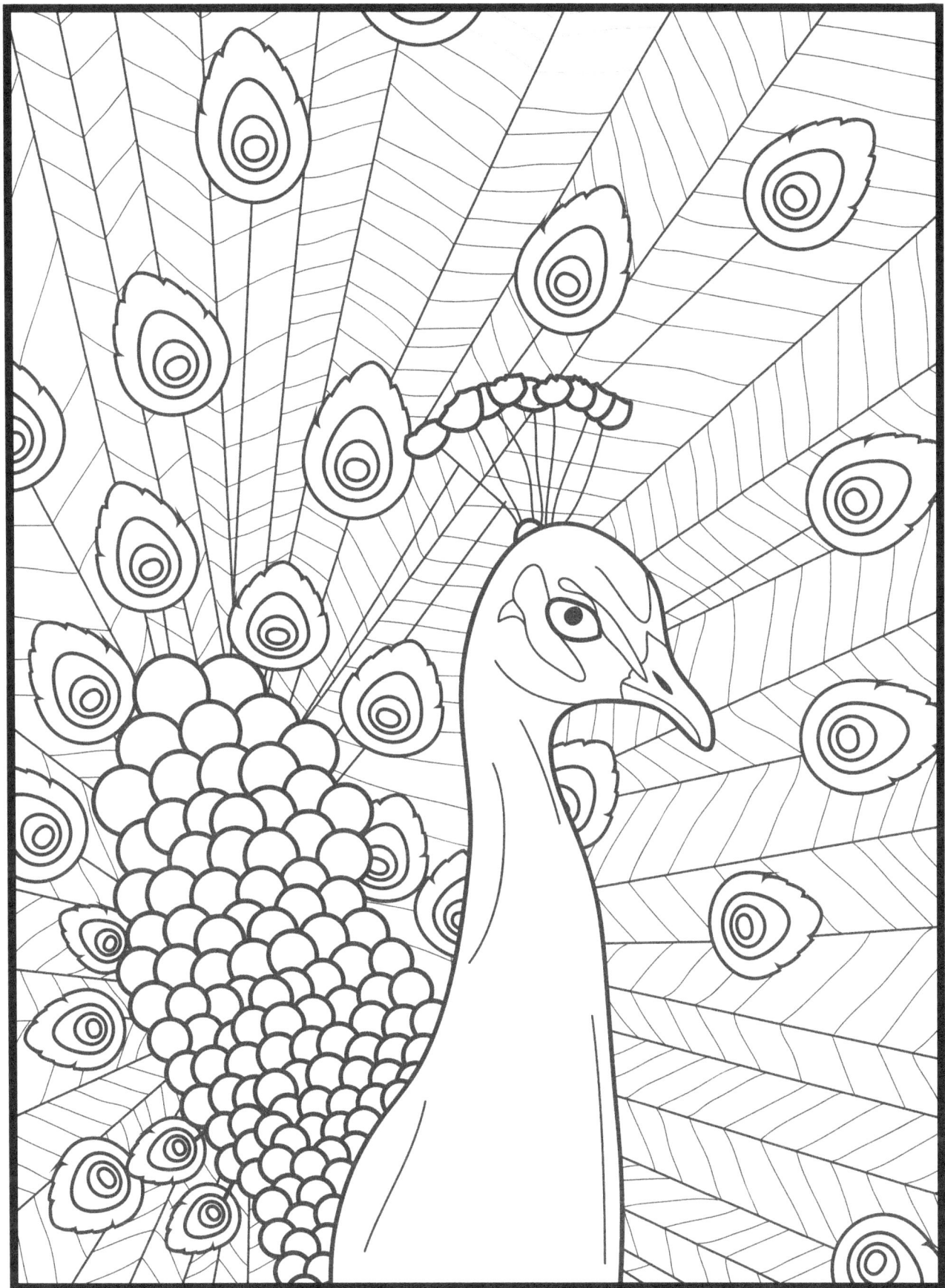

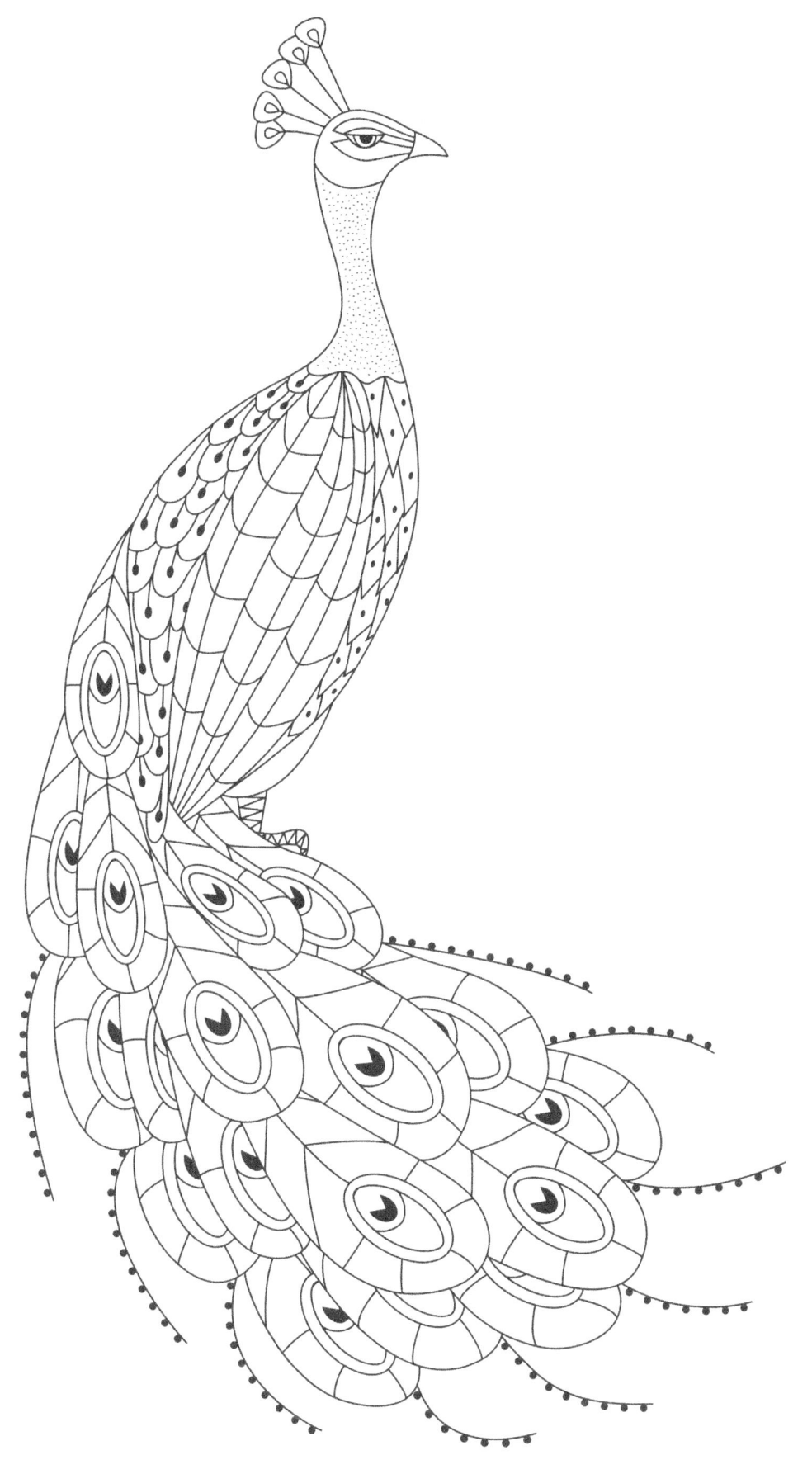

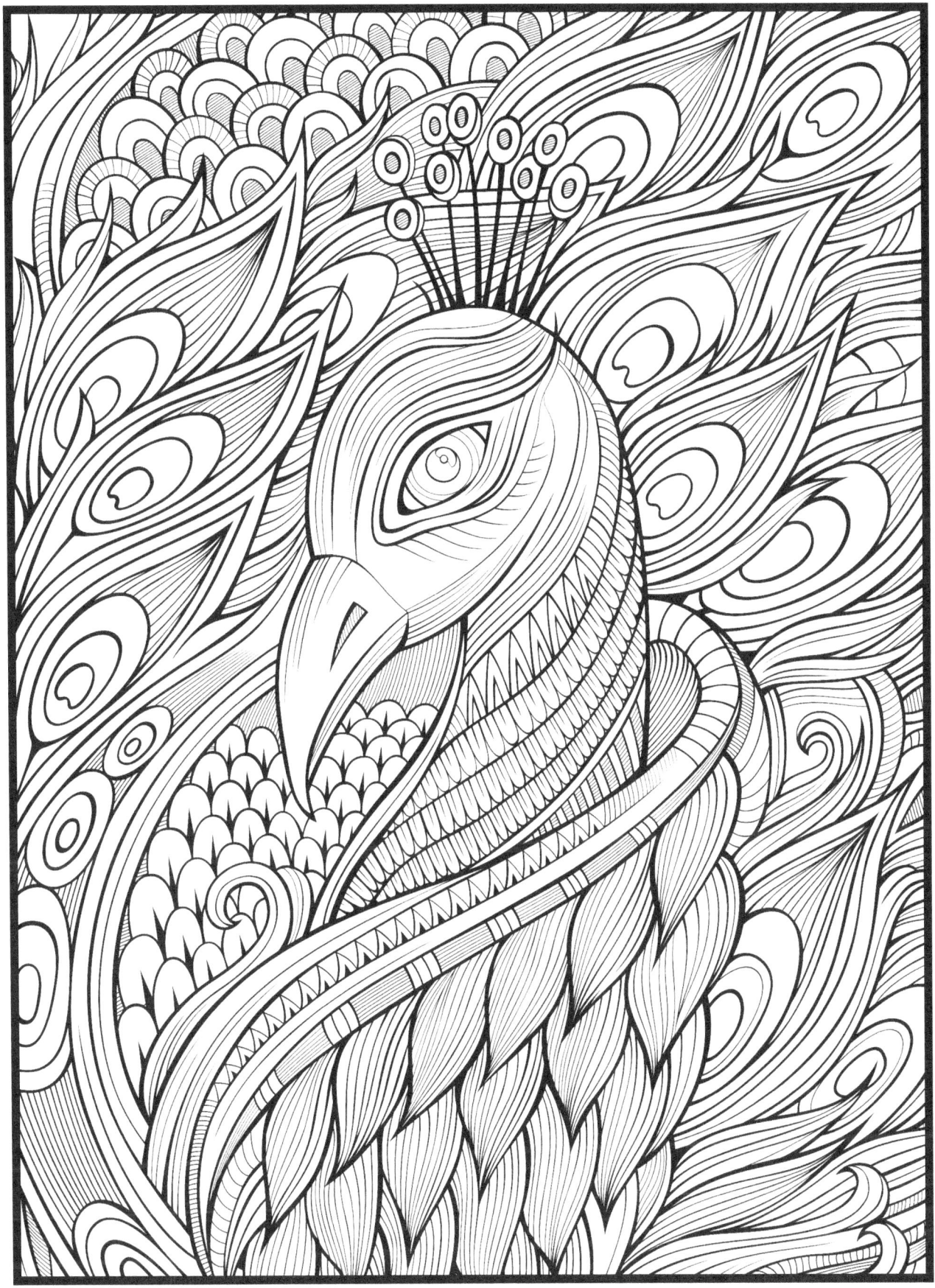

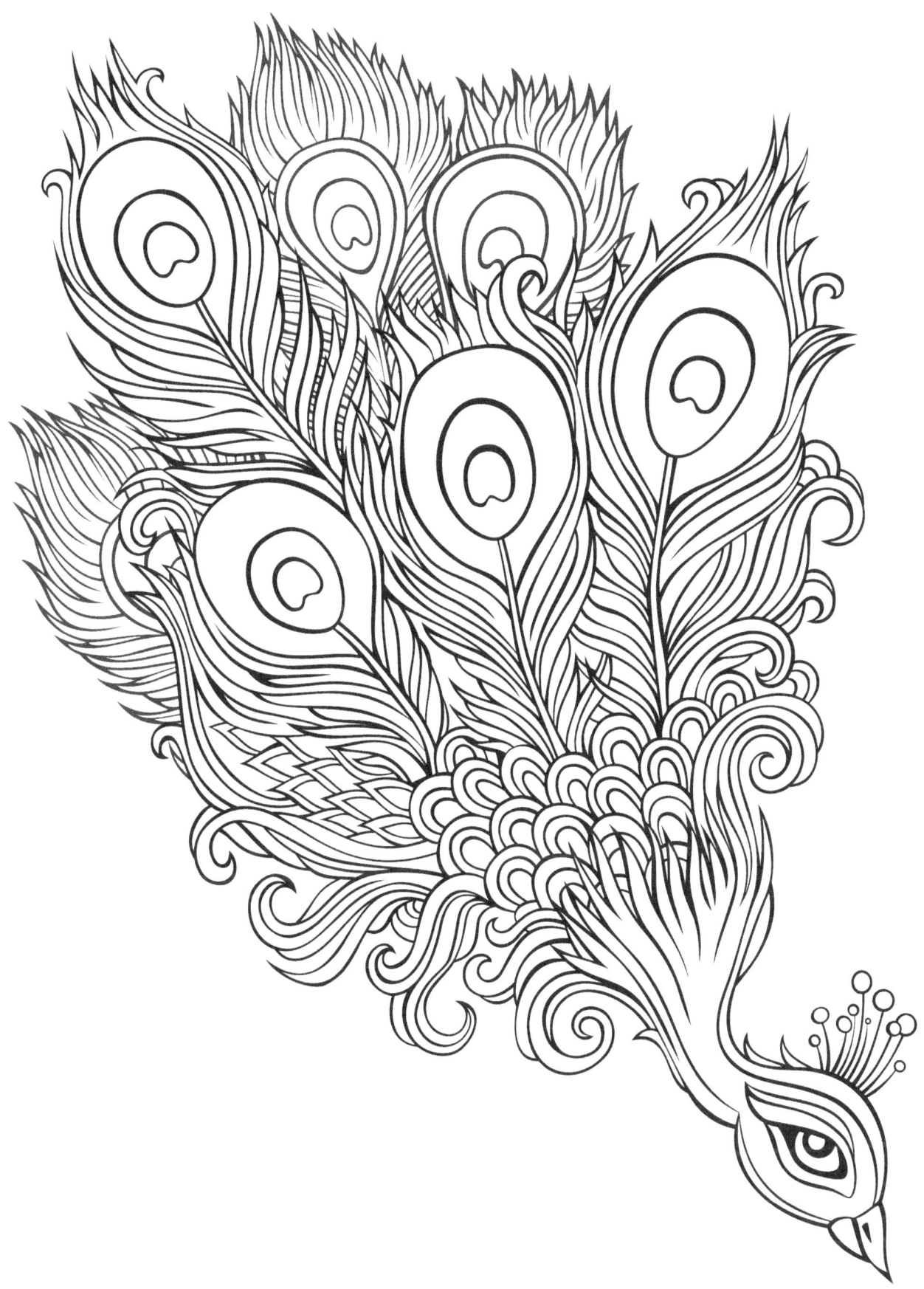

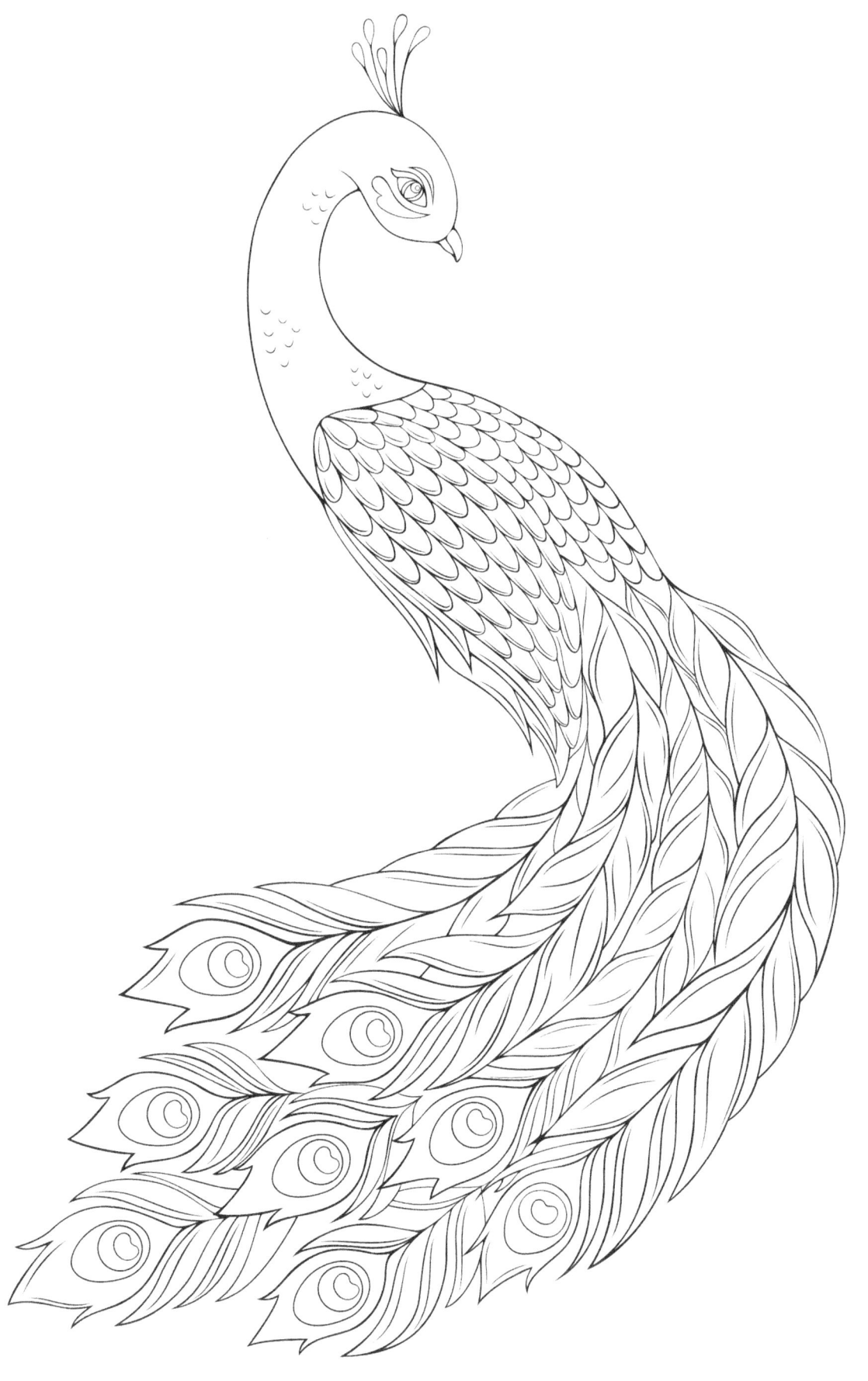

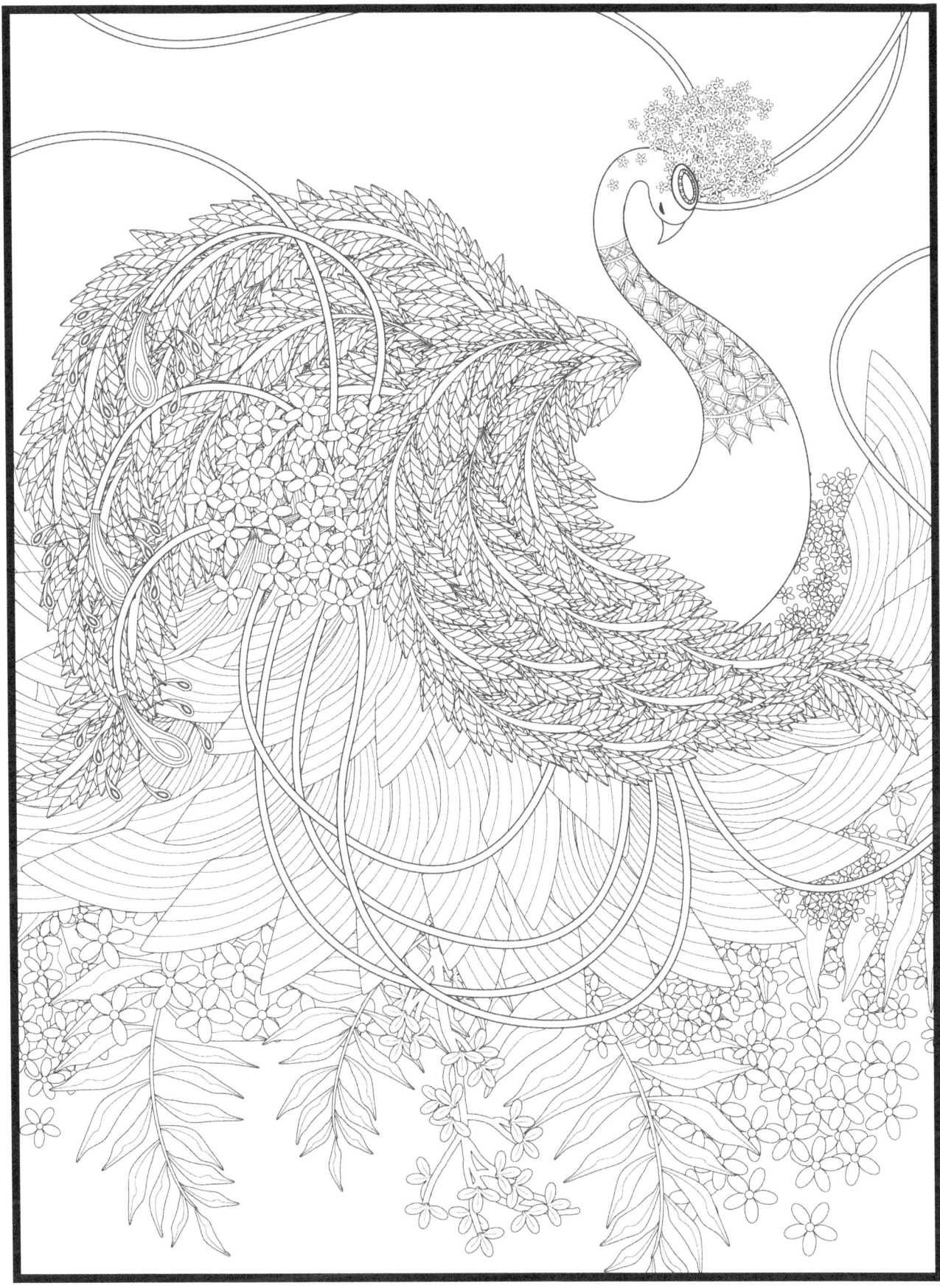

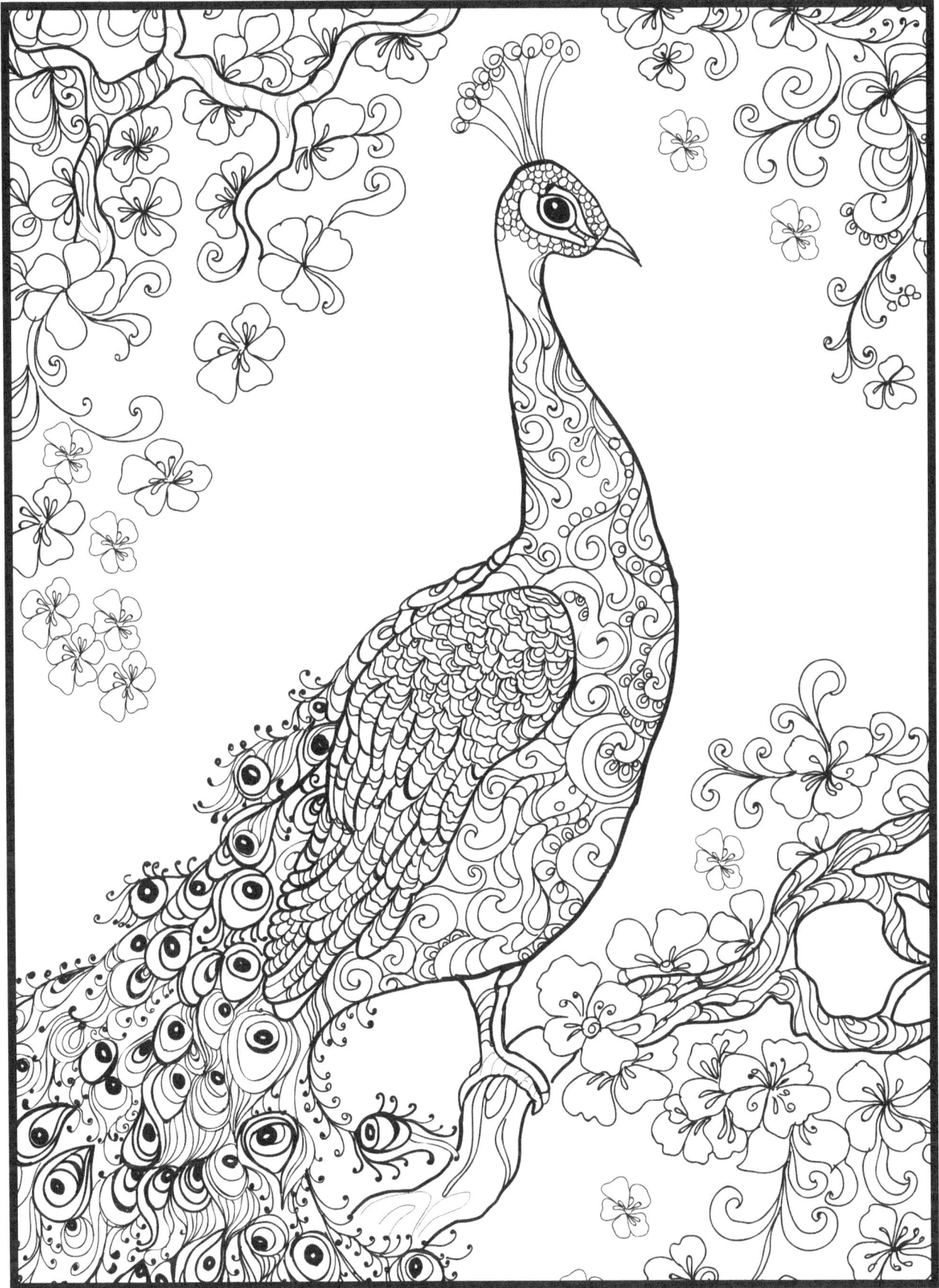

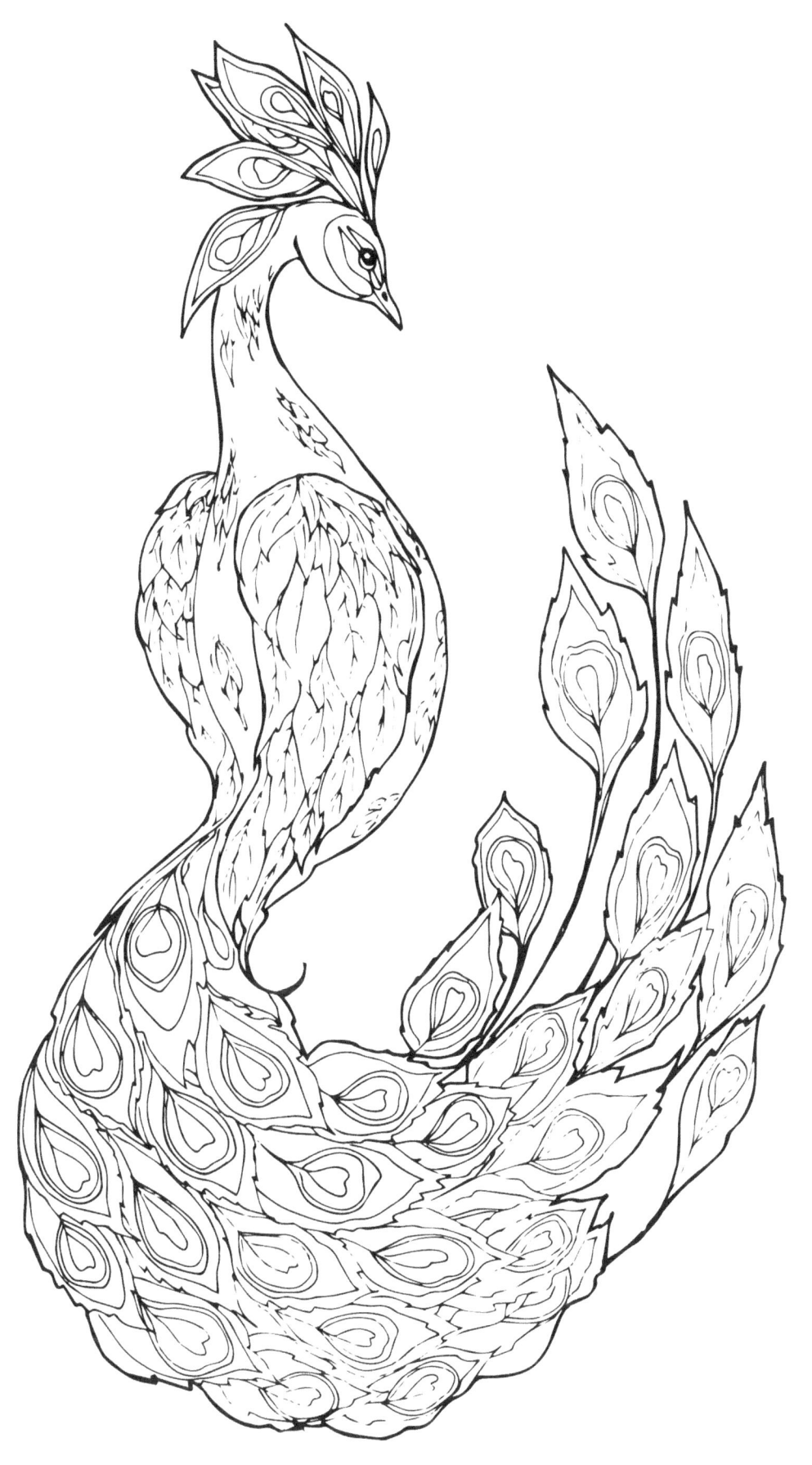

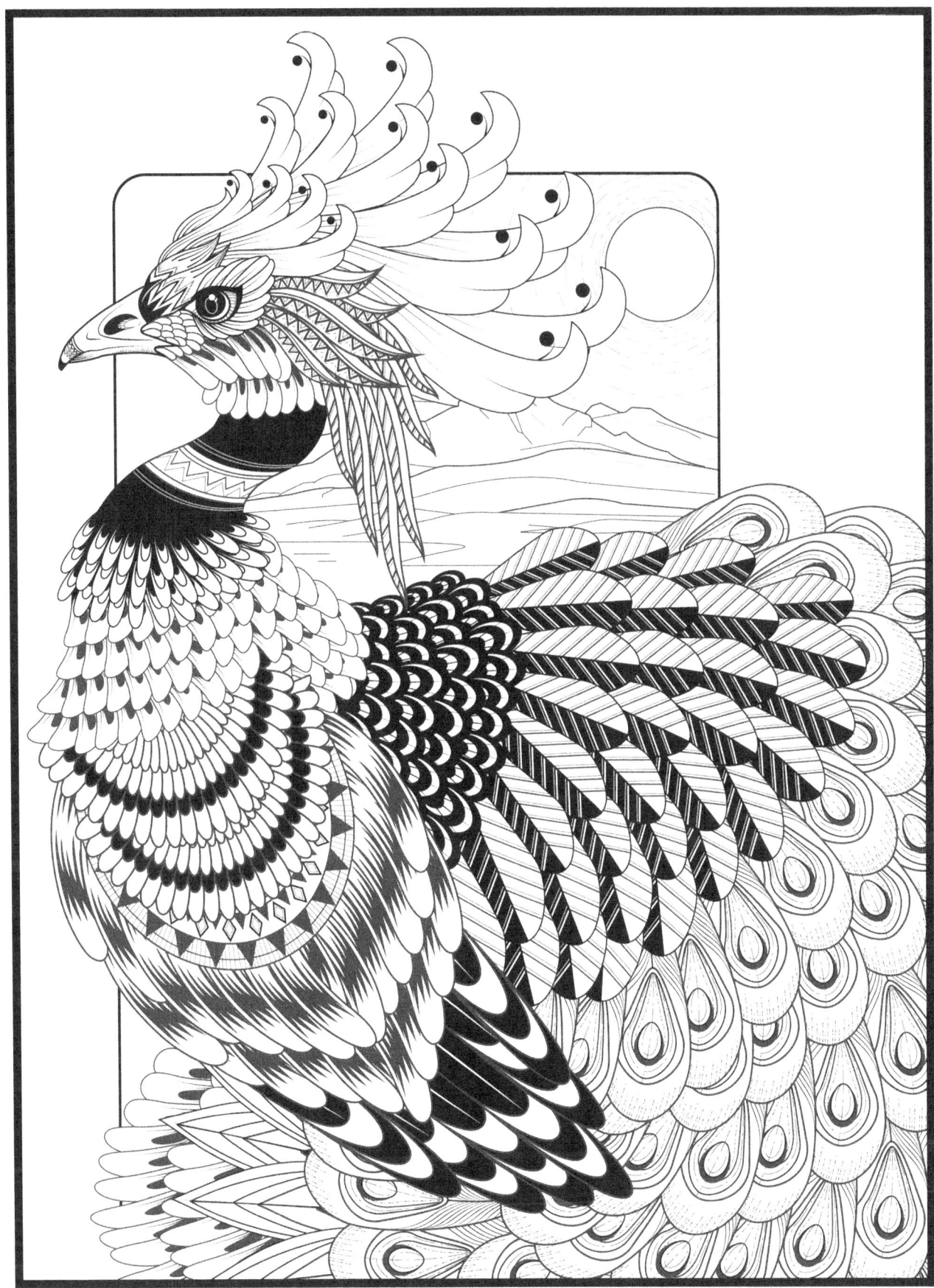

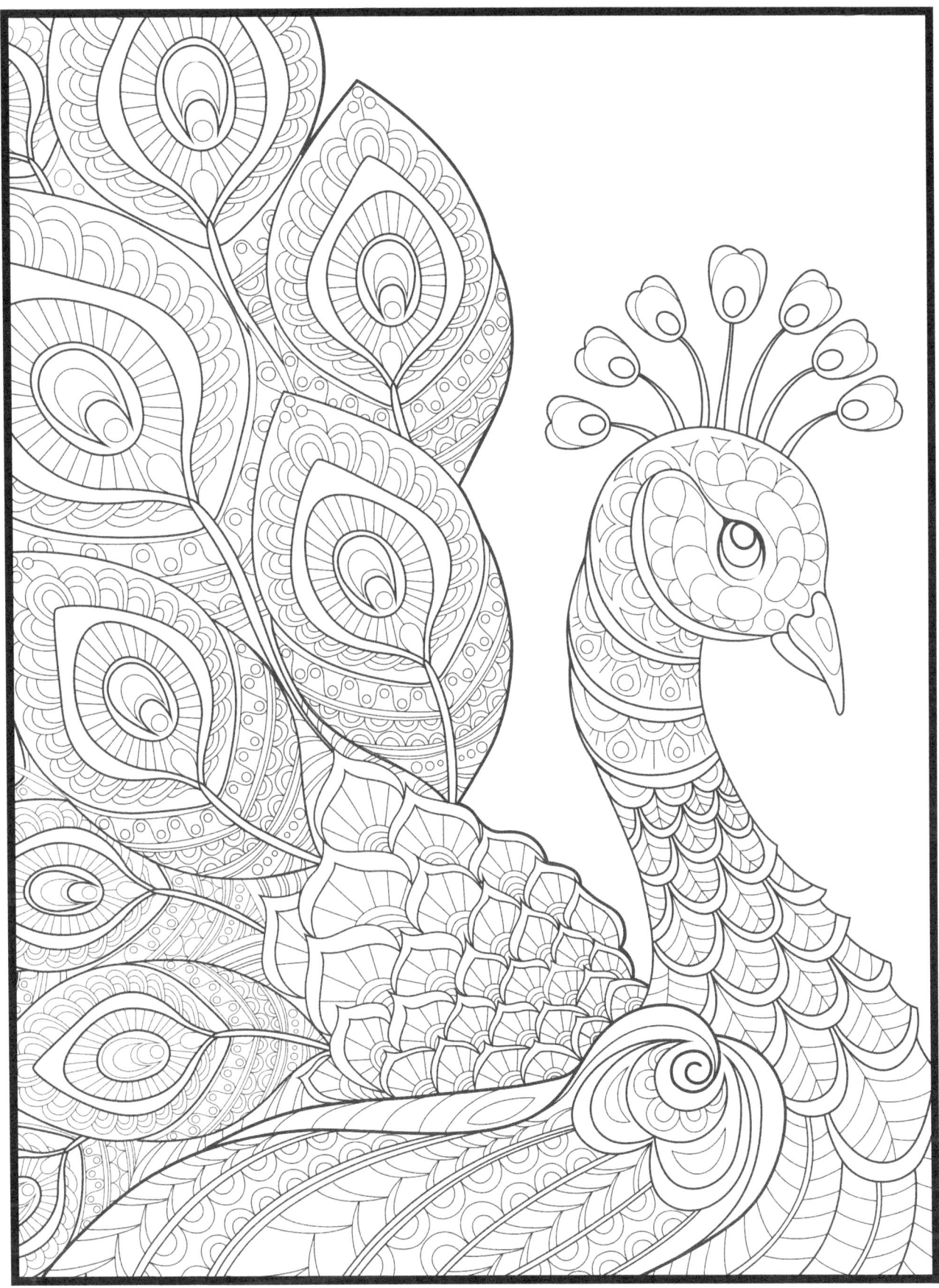

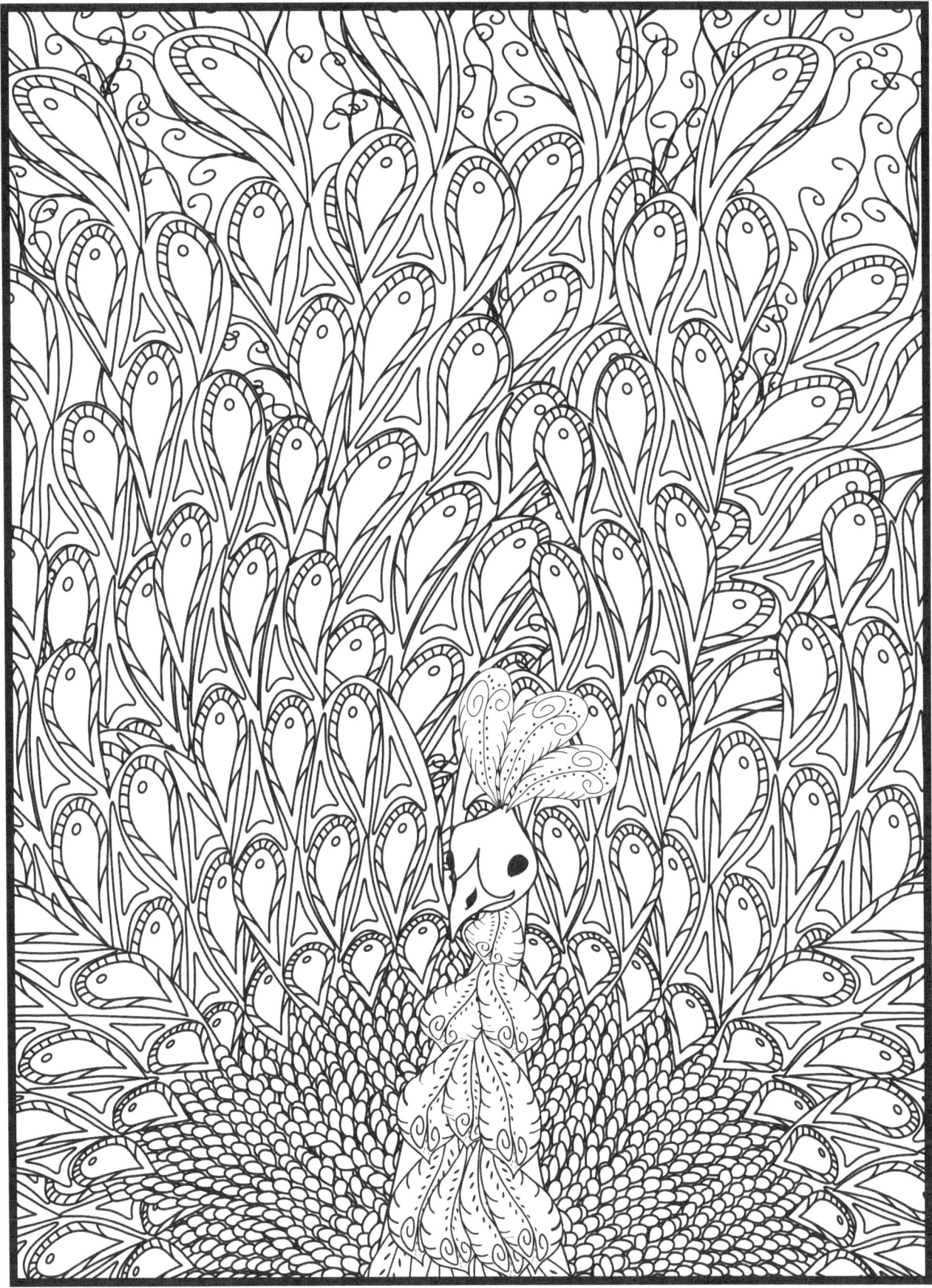

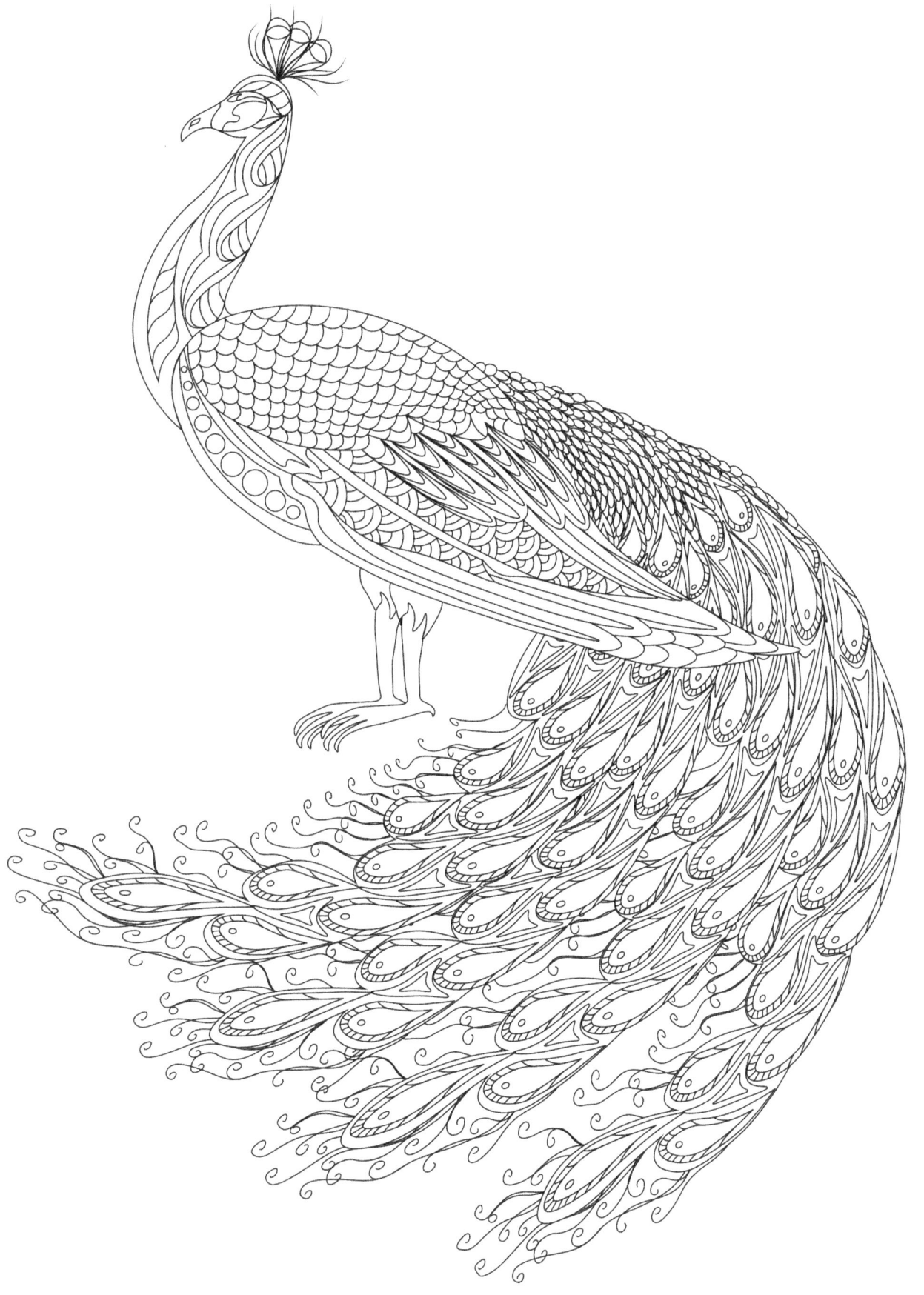

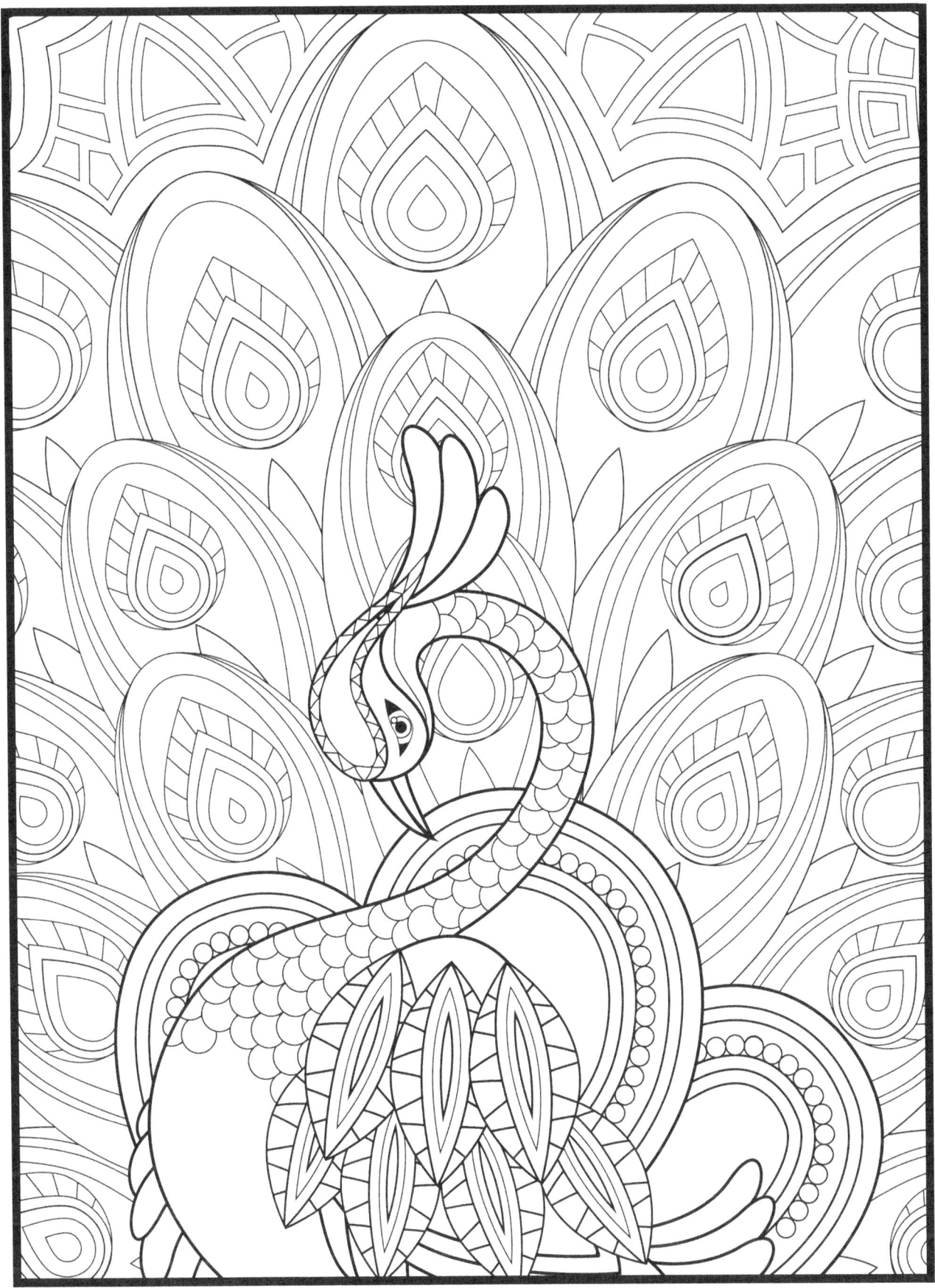

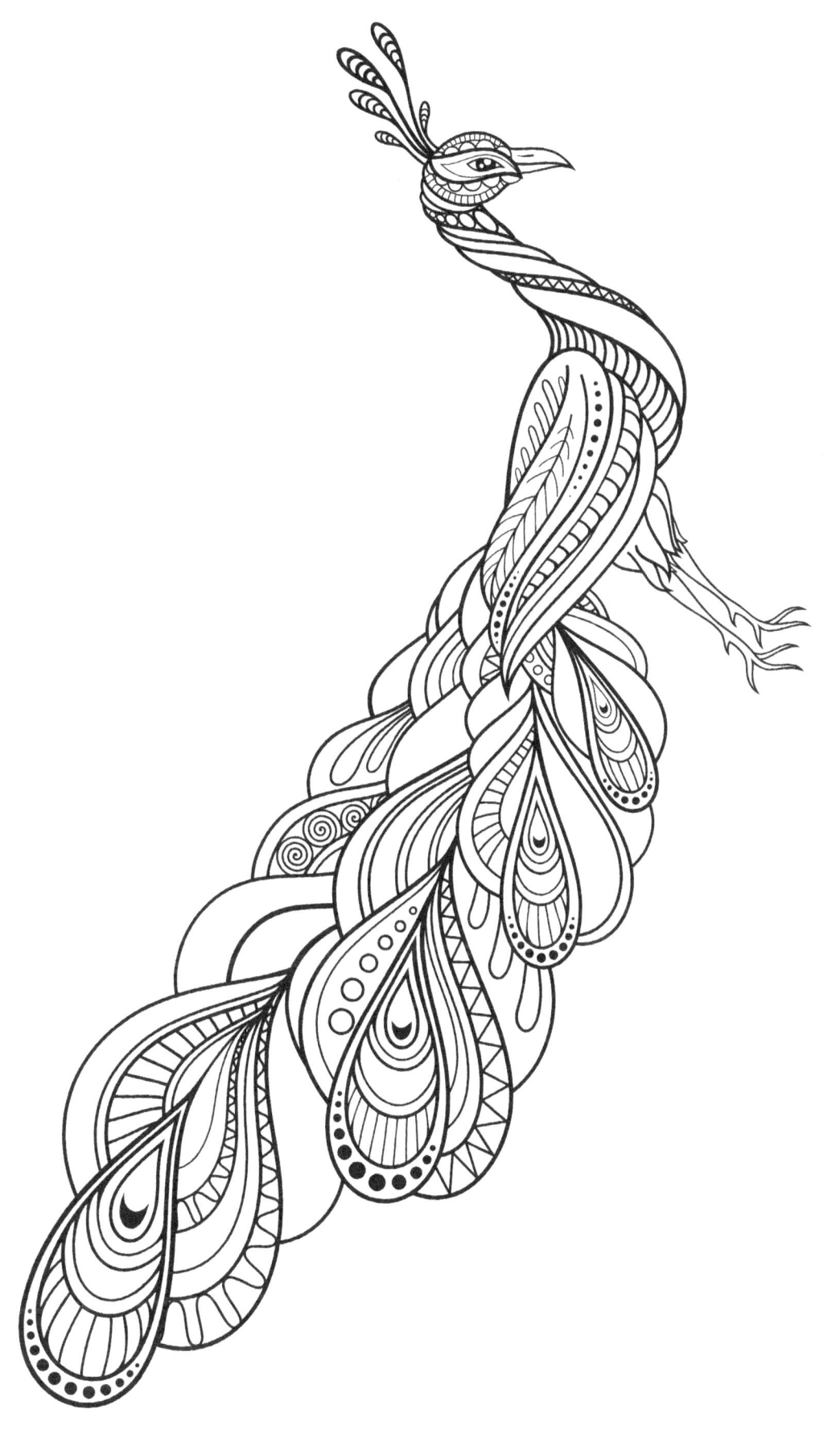

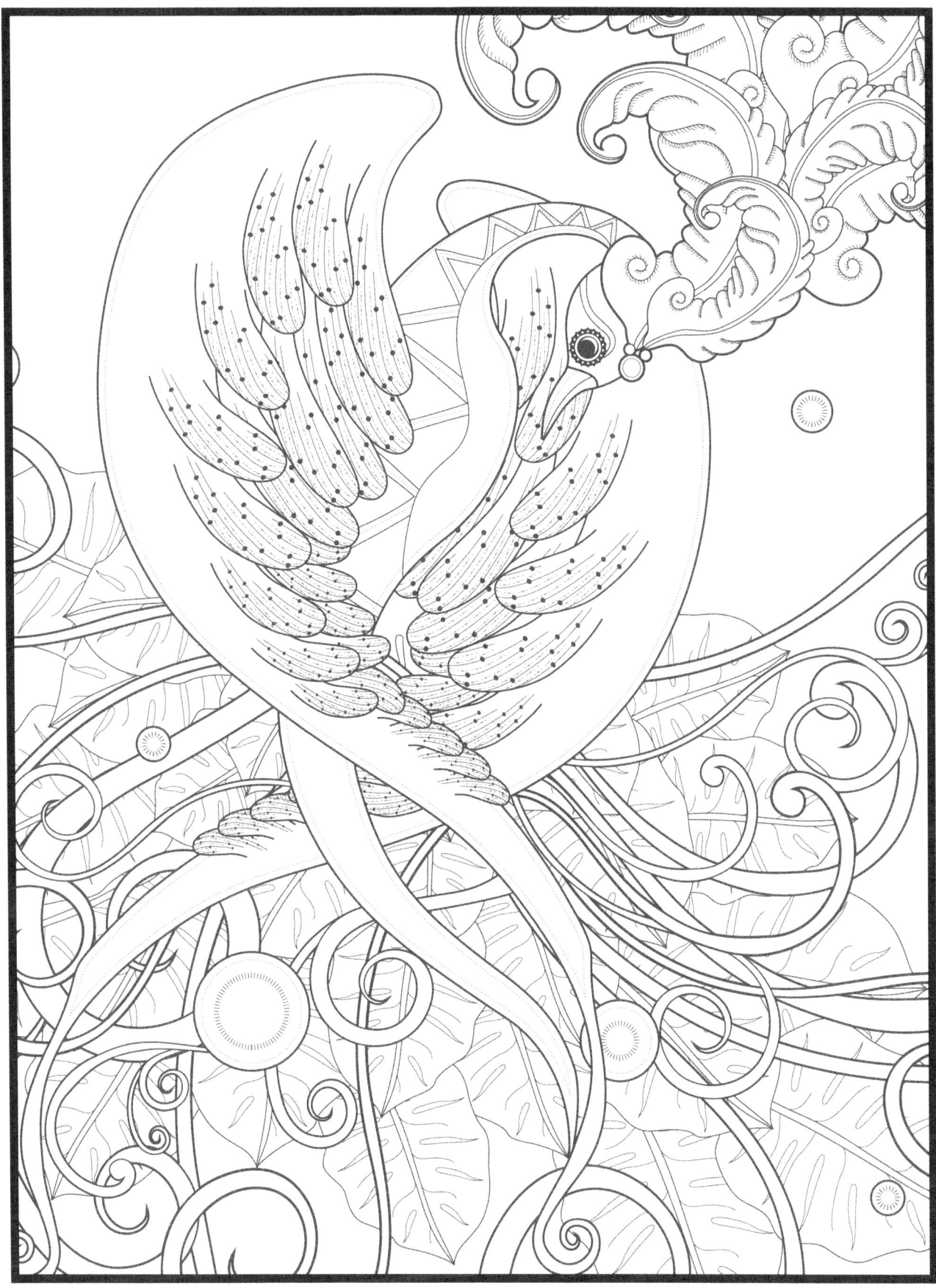

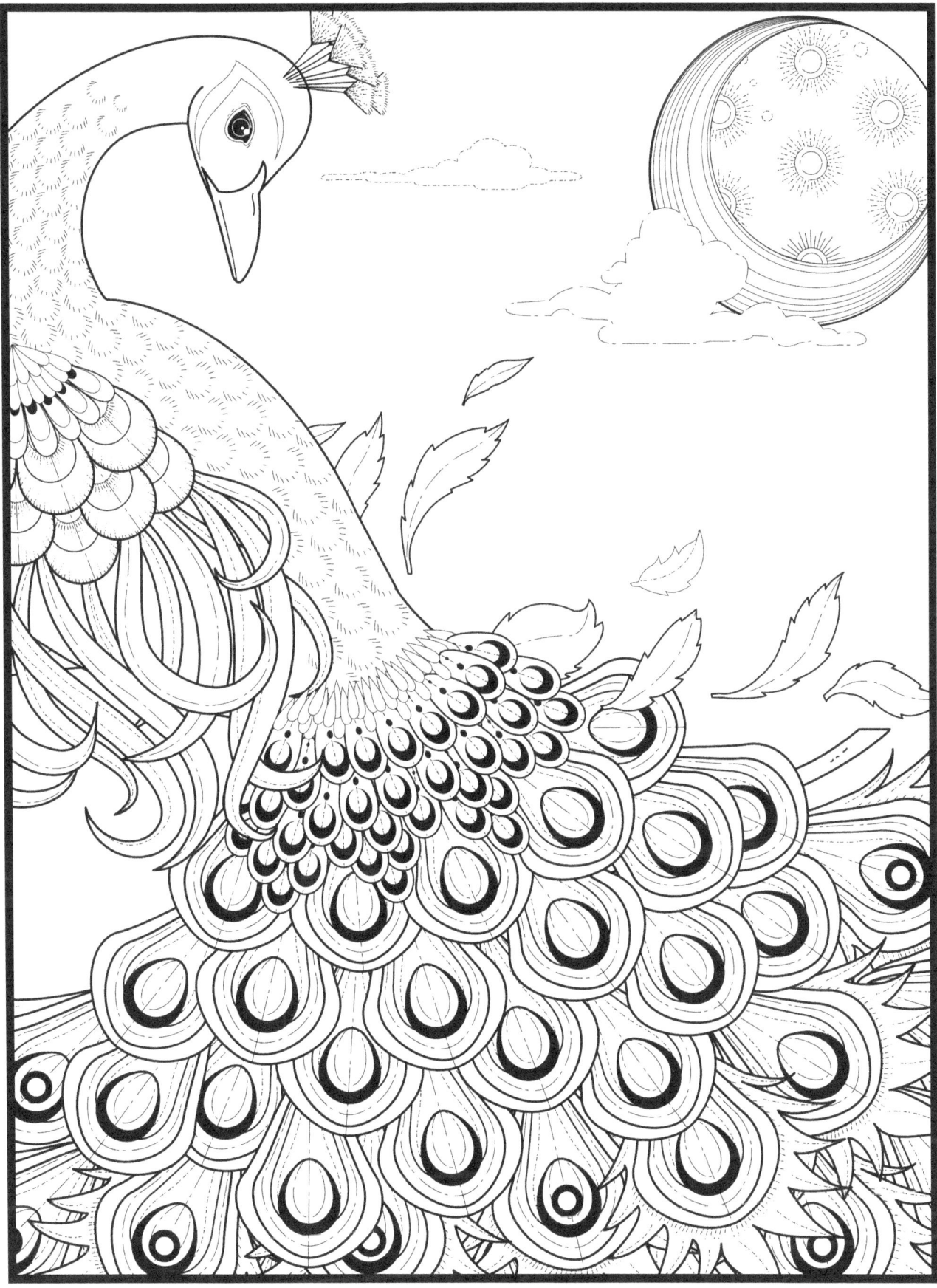

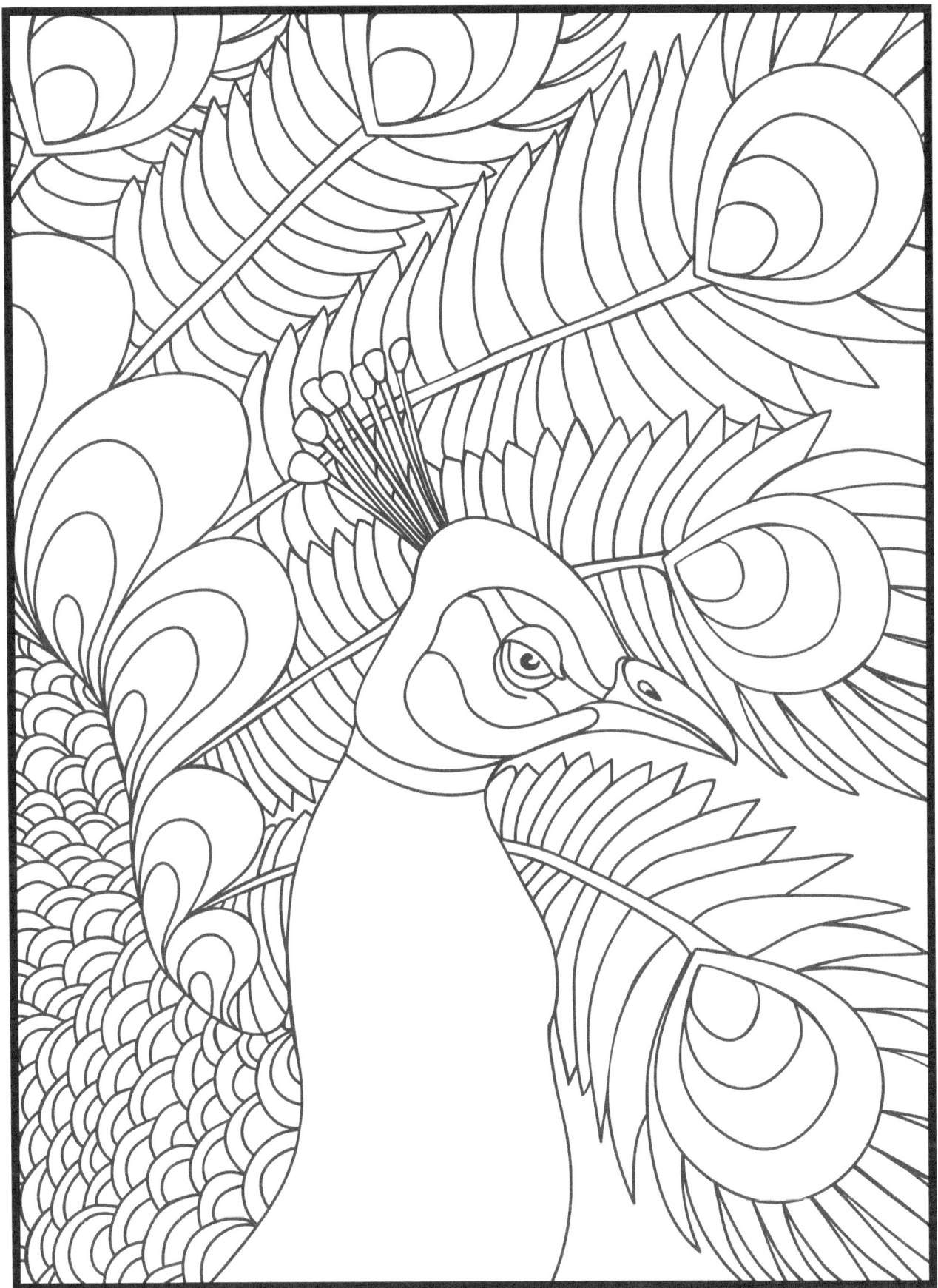

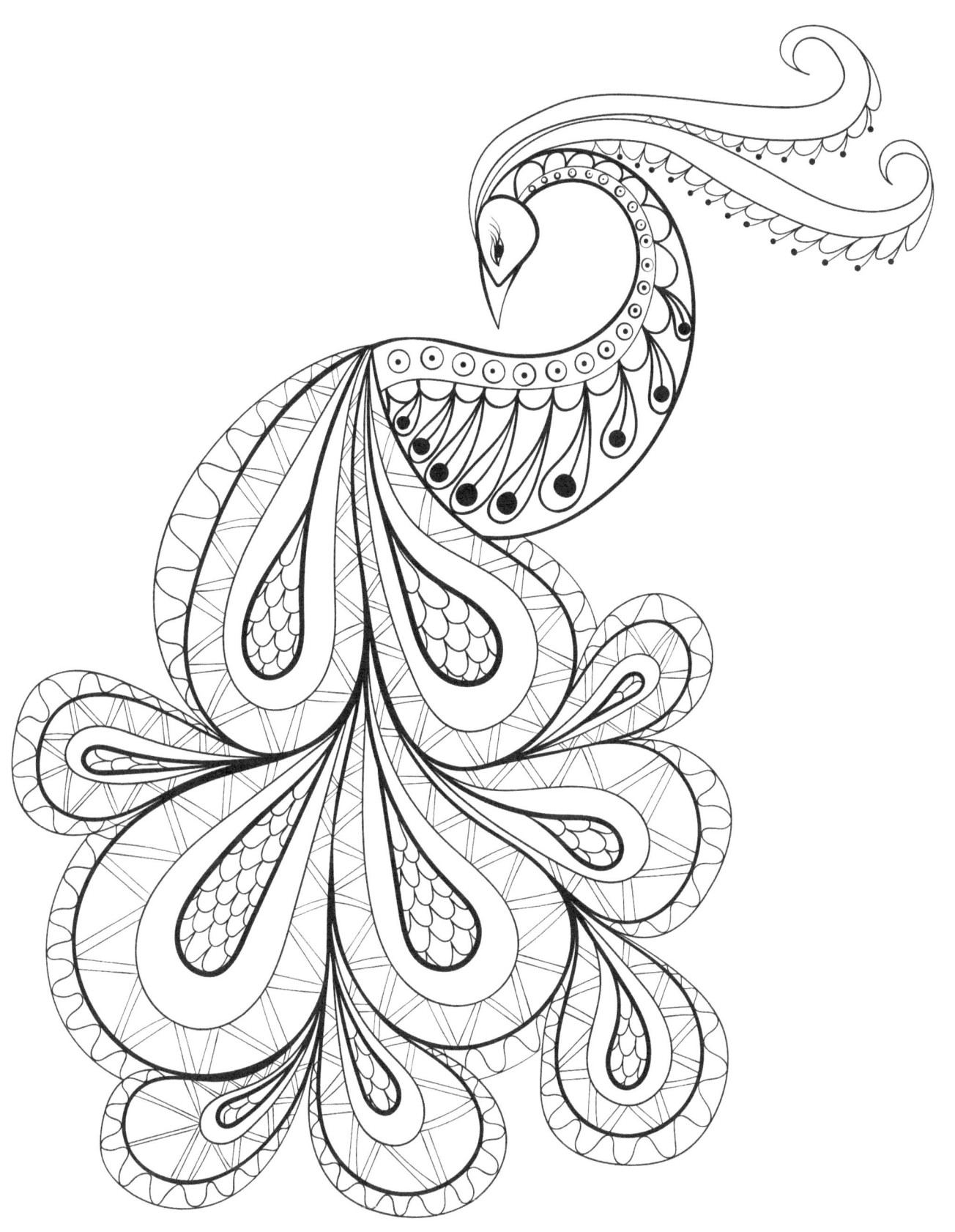

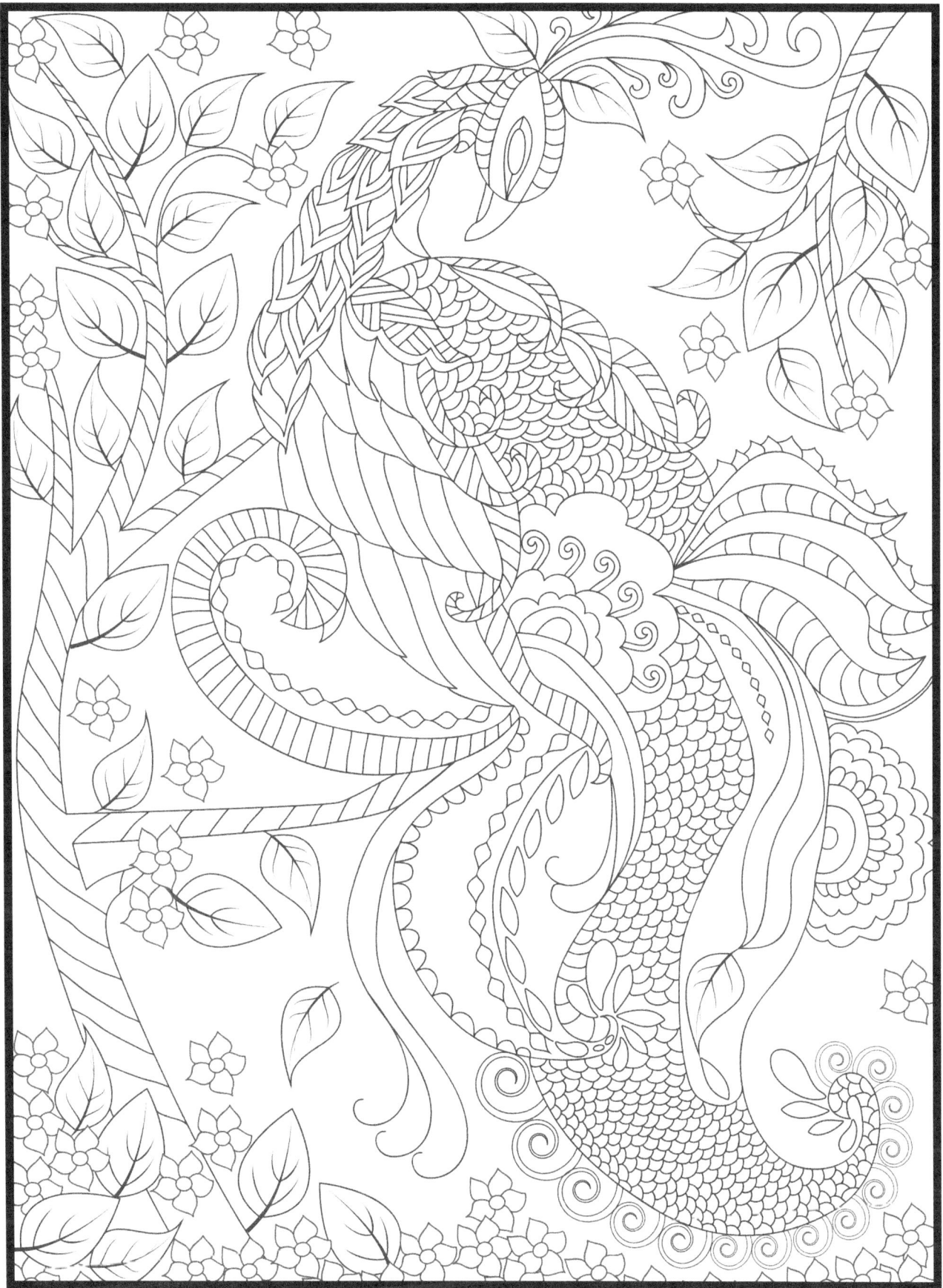

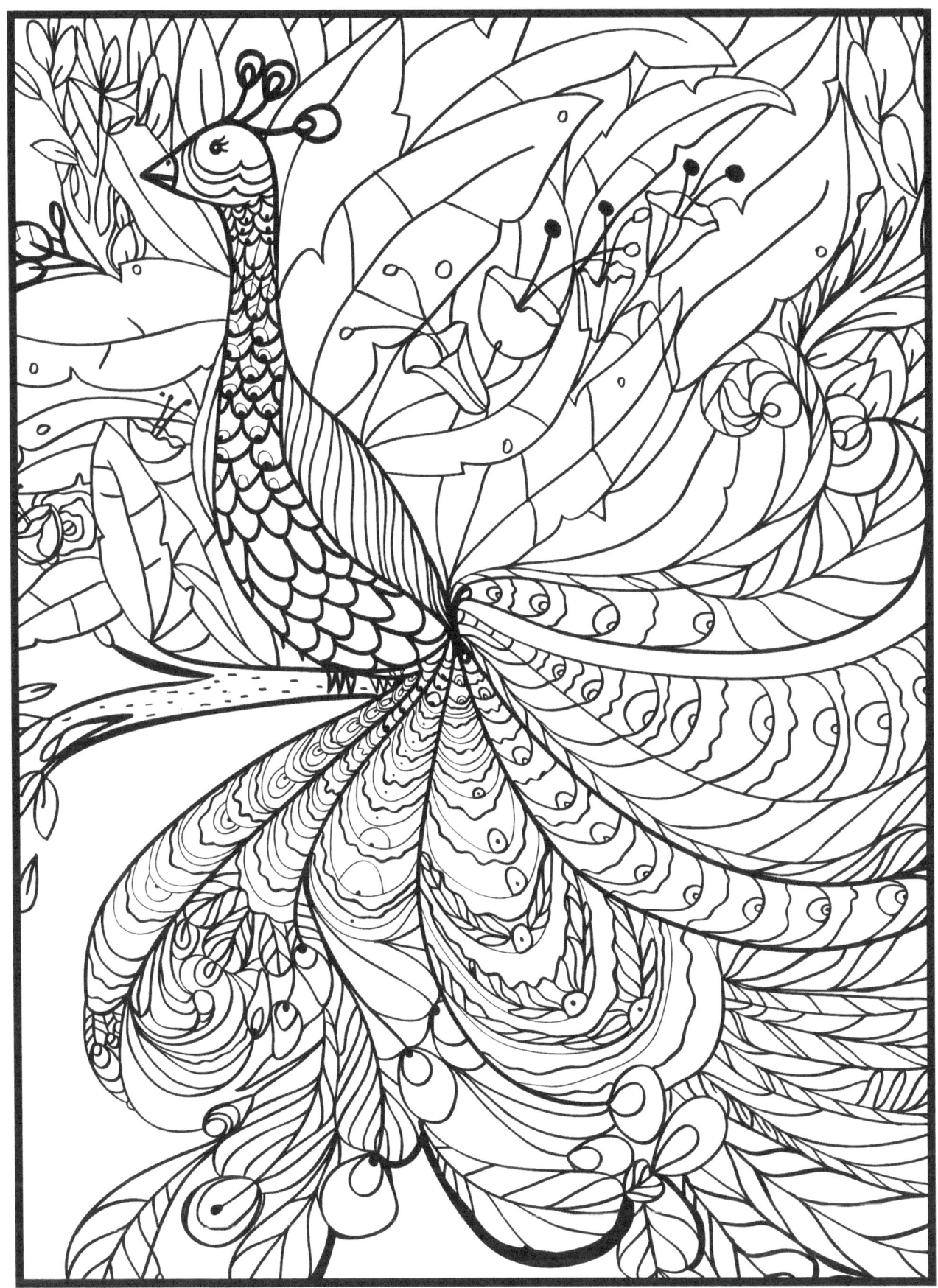

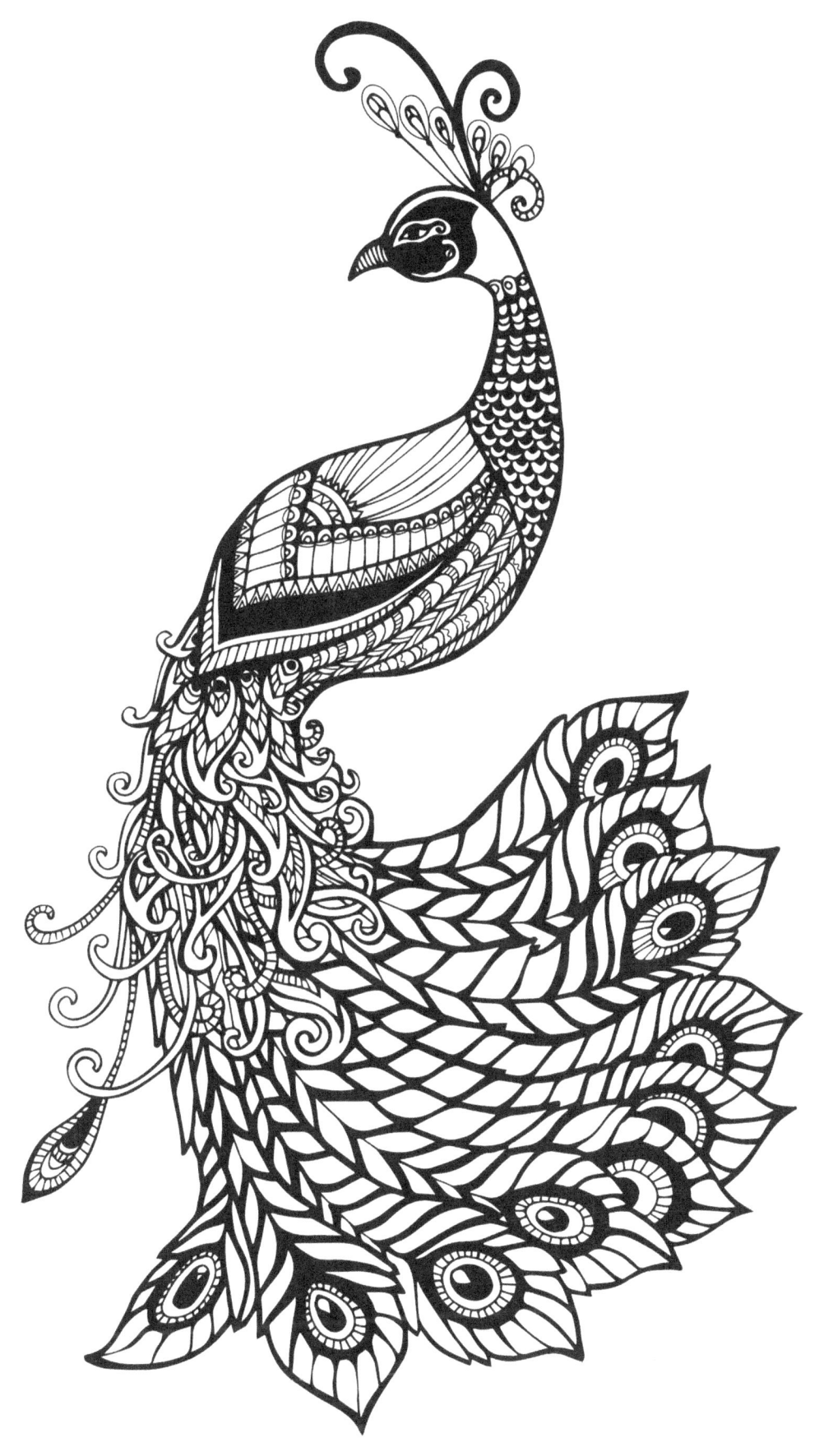

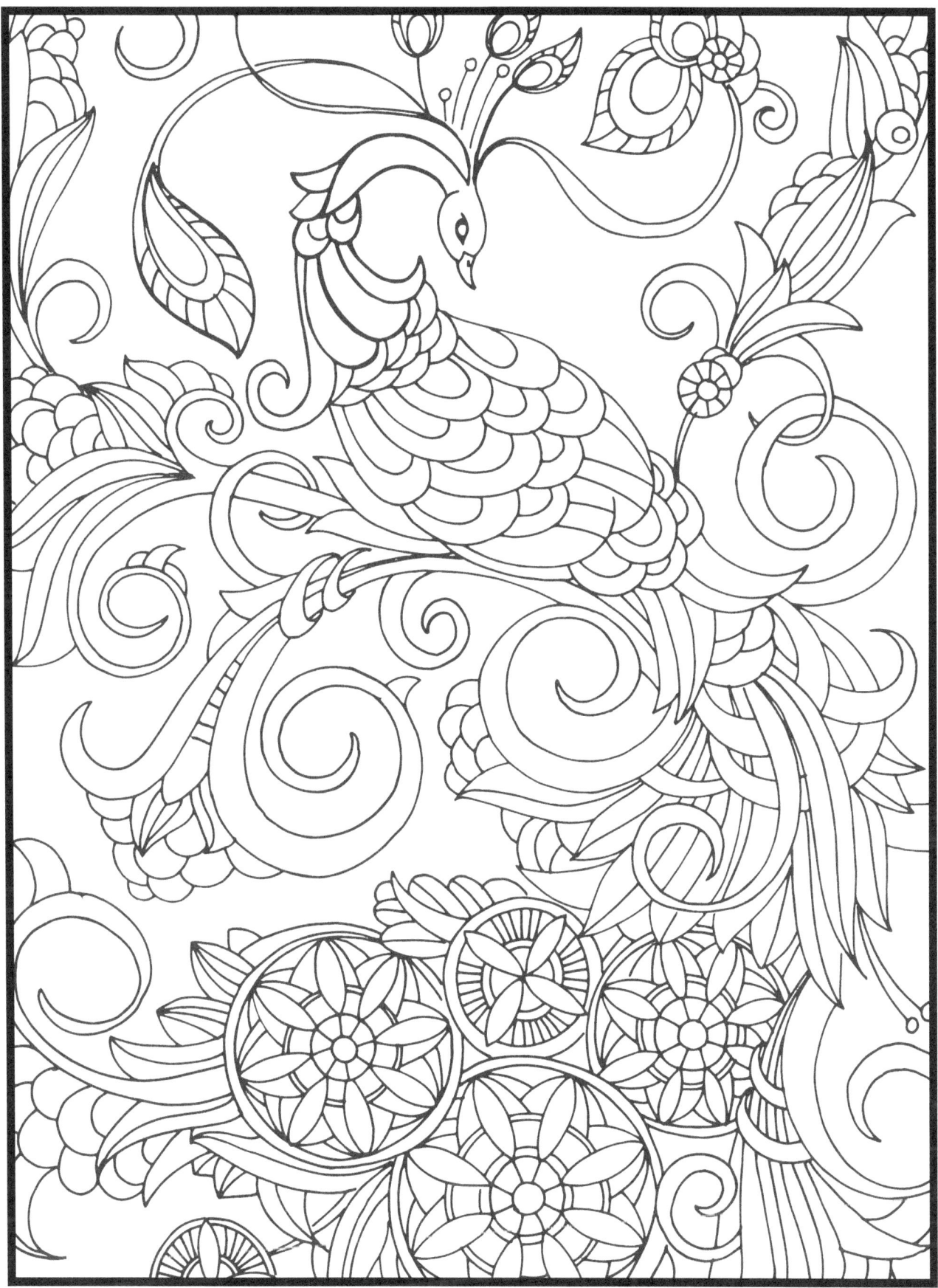

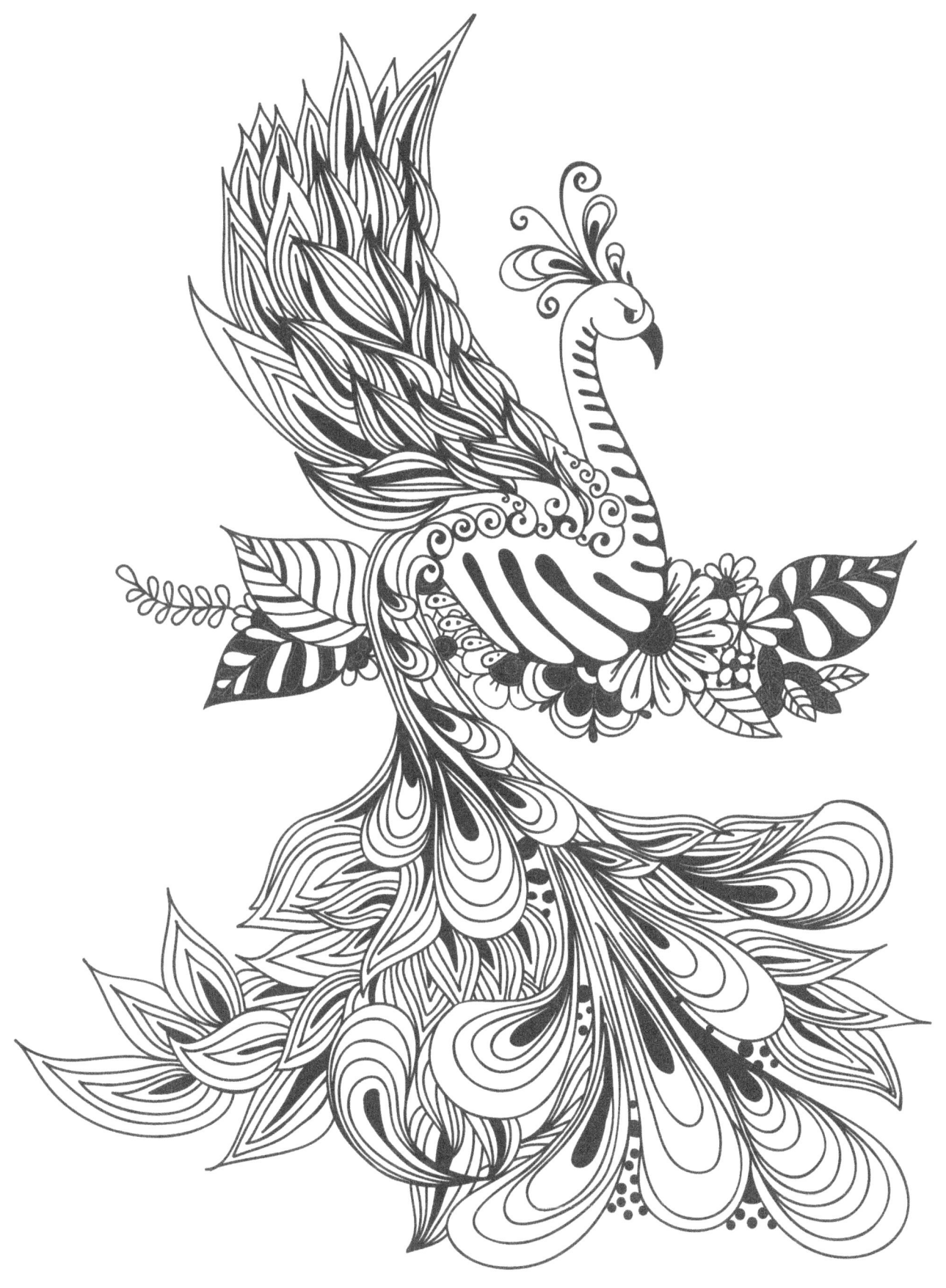

.

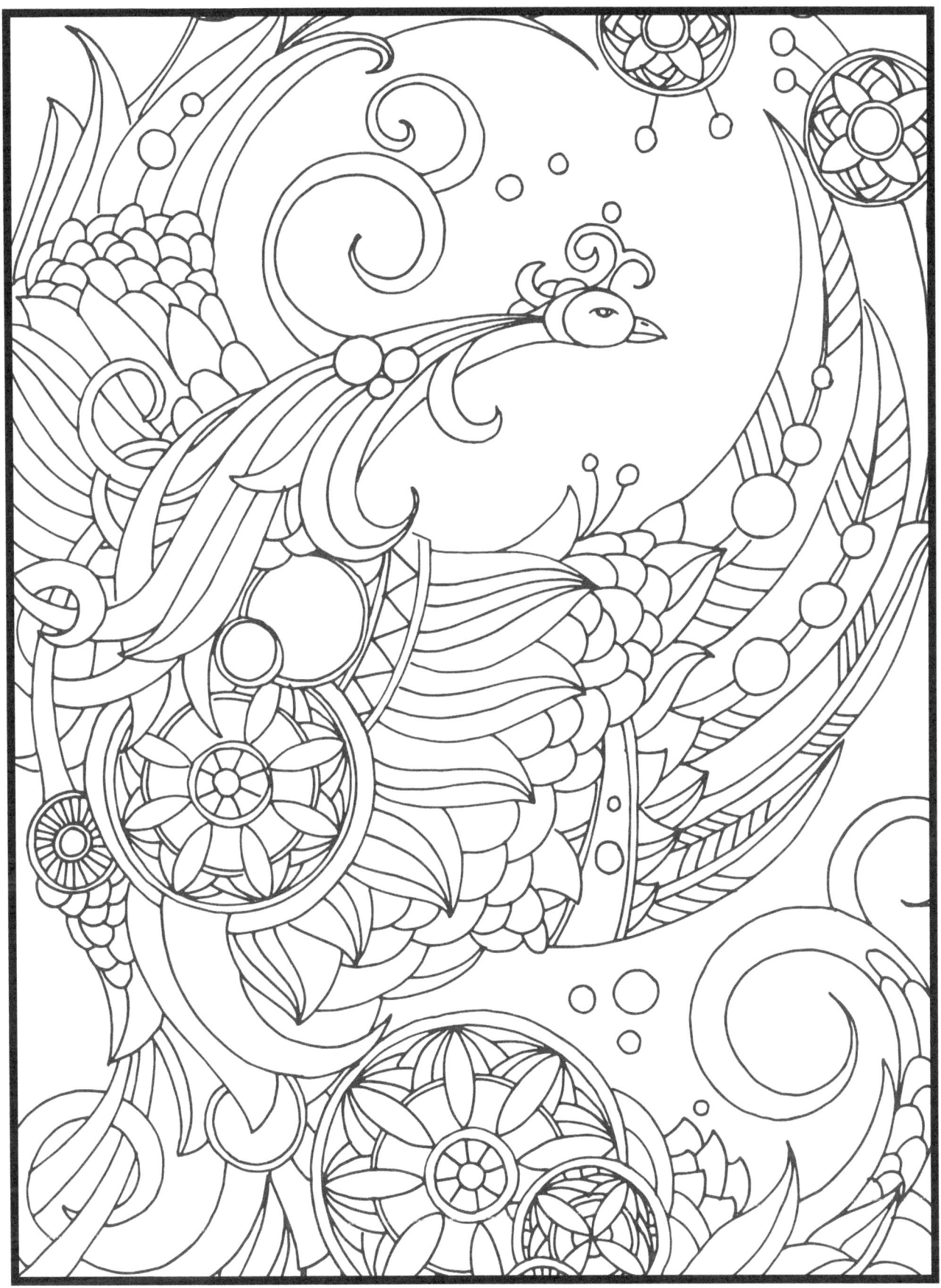

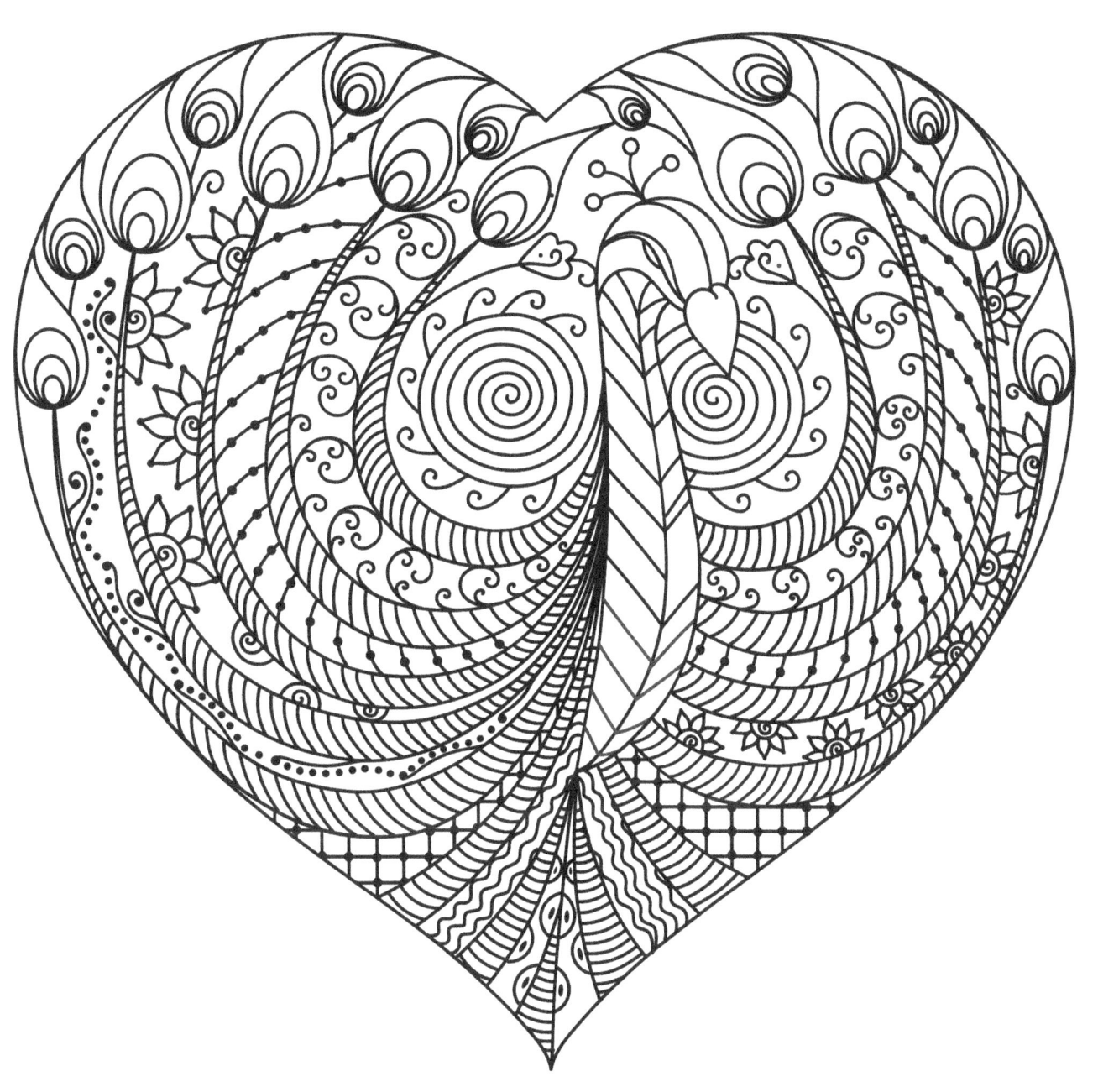

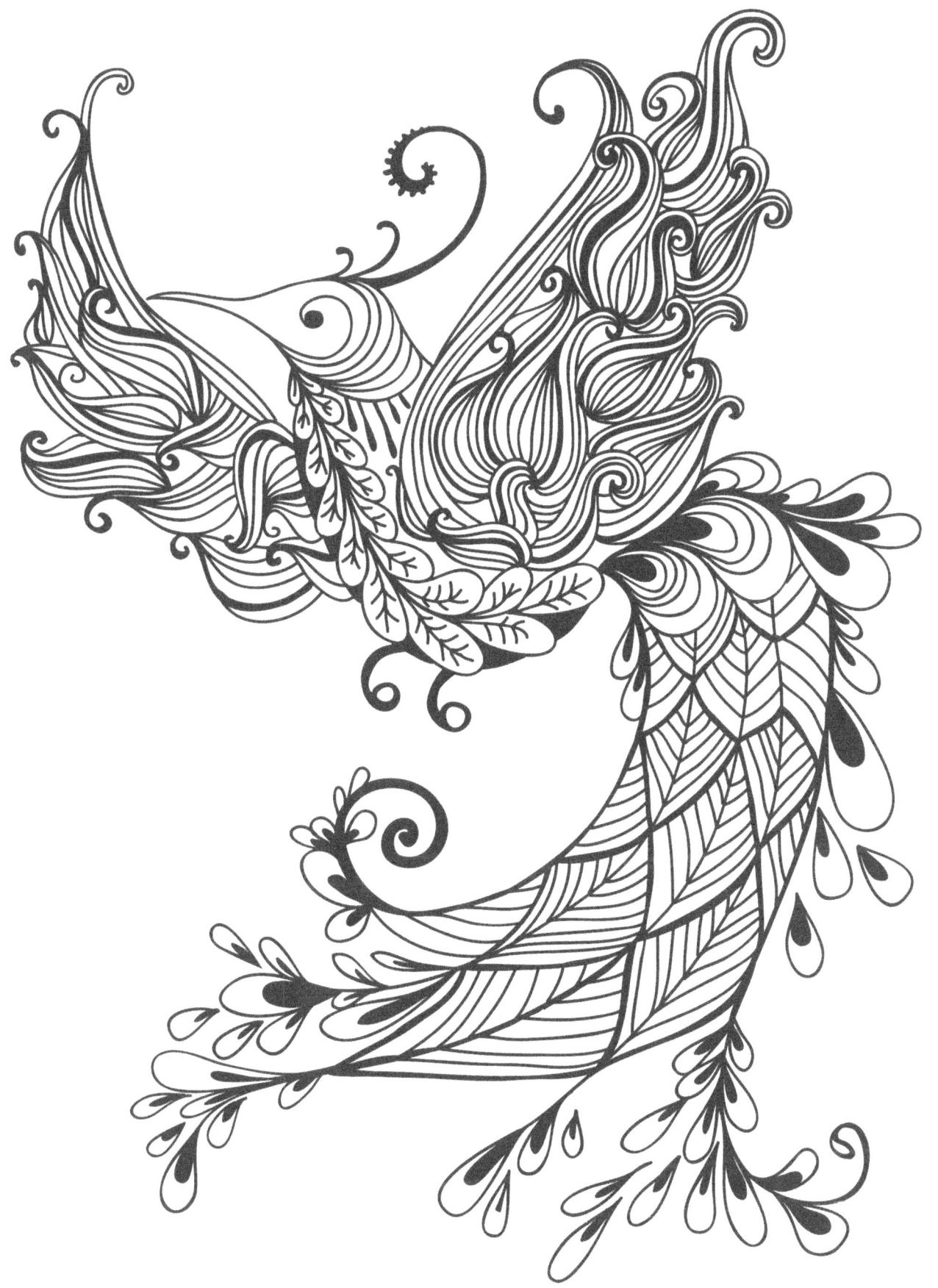

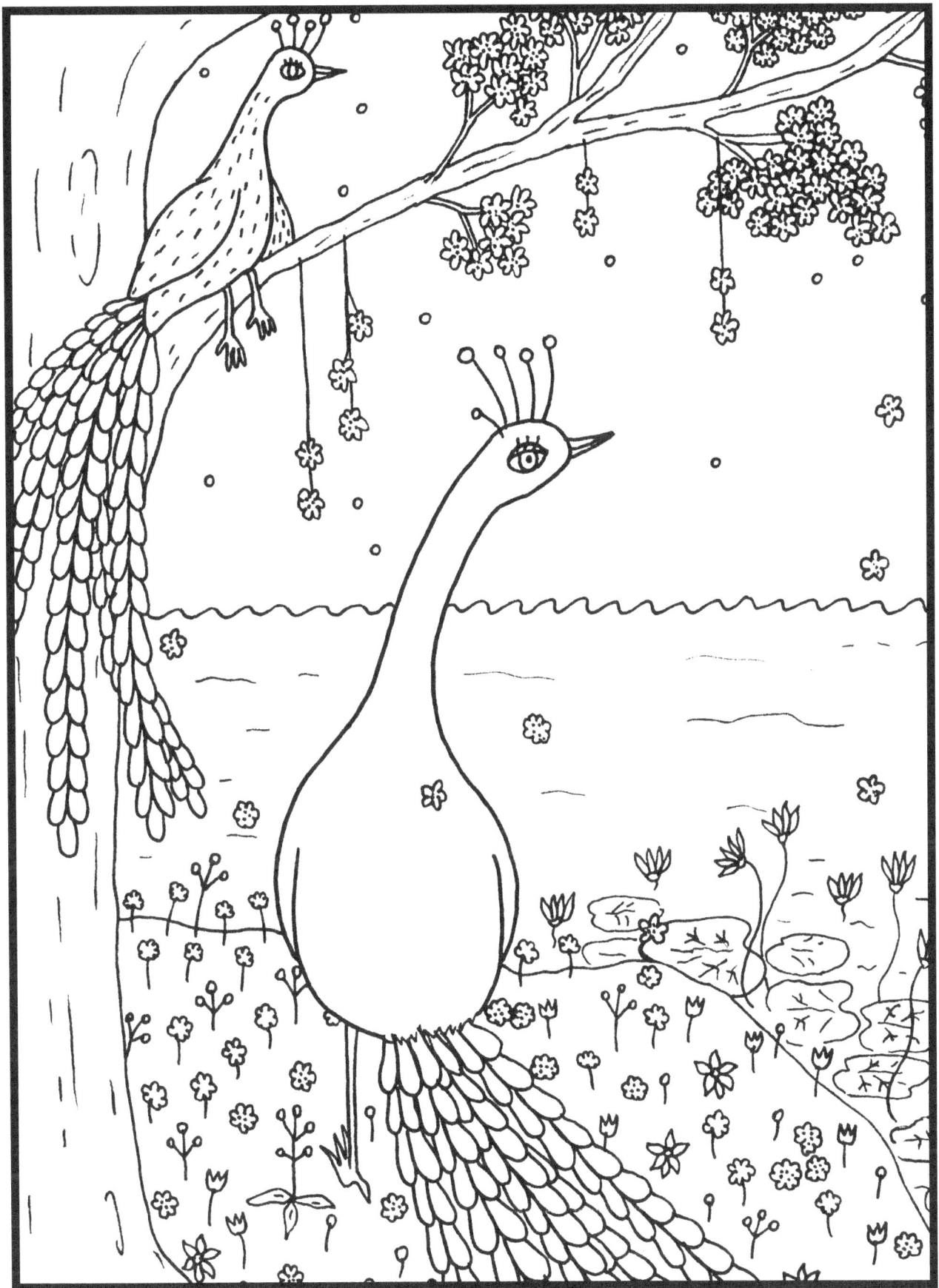

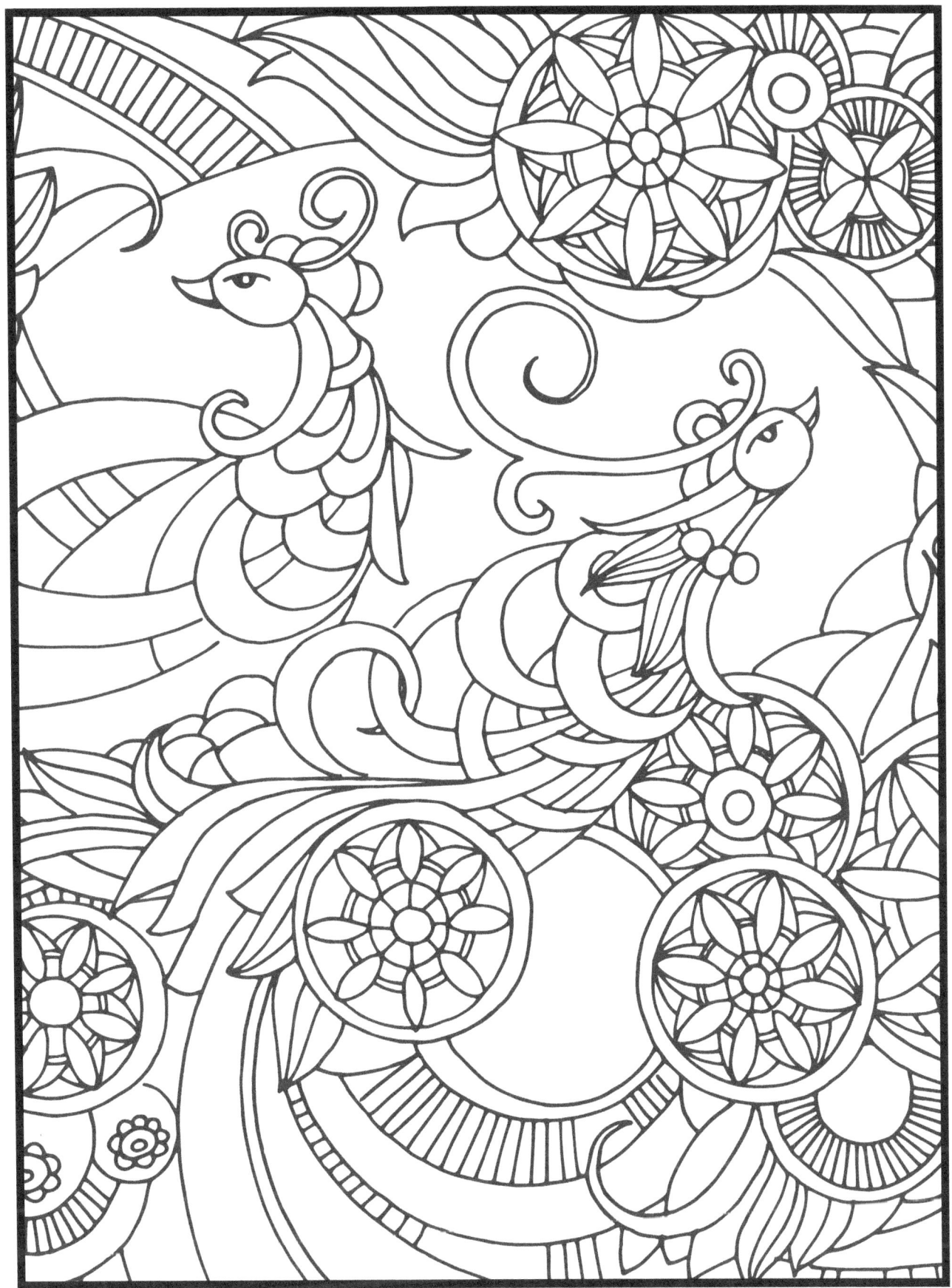

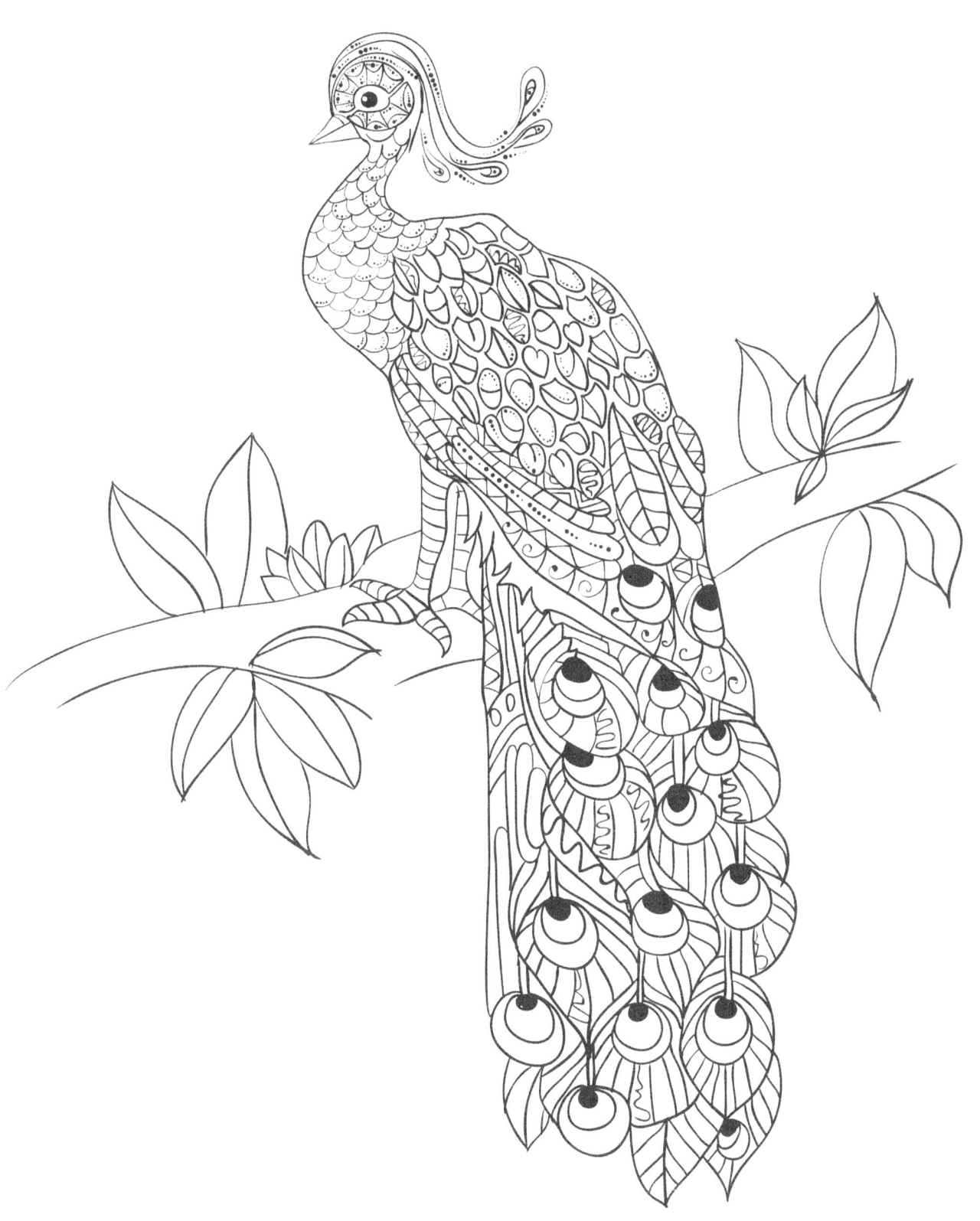

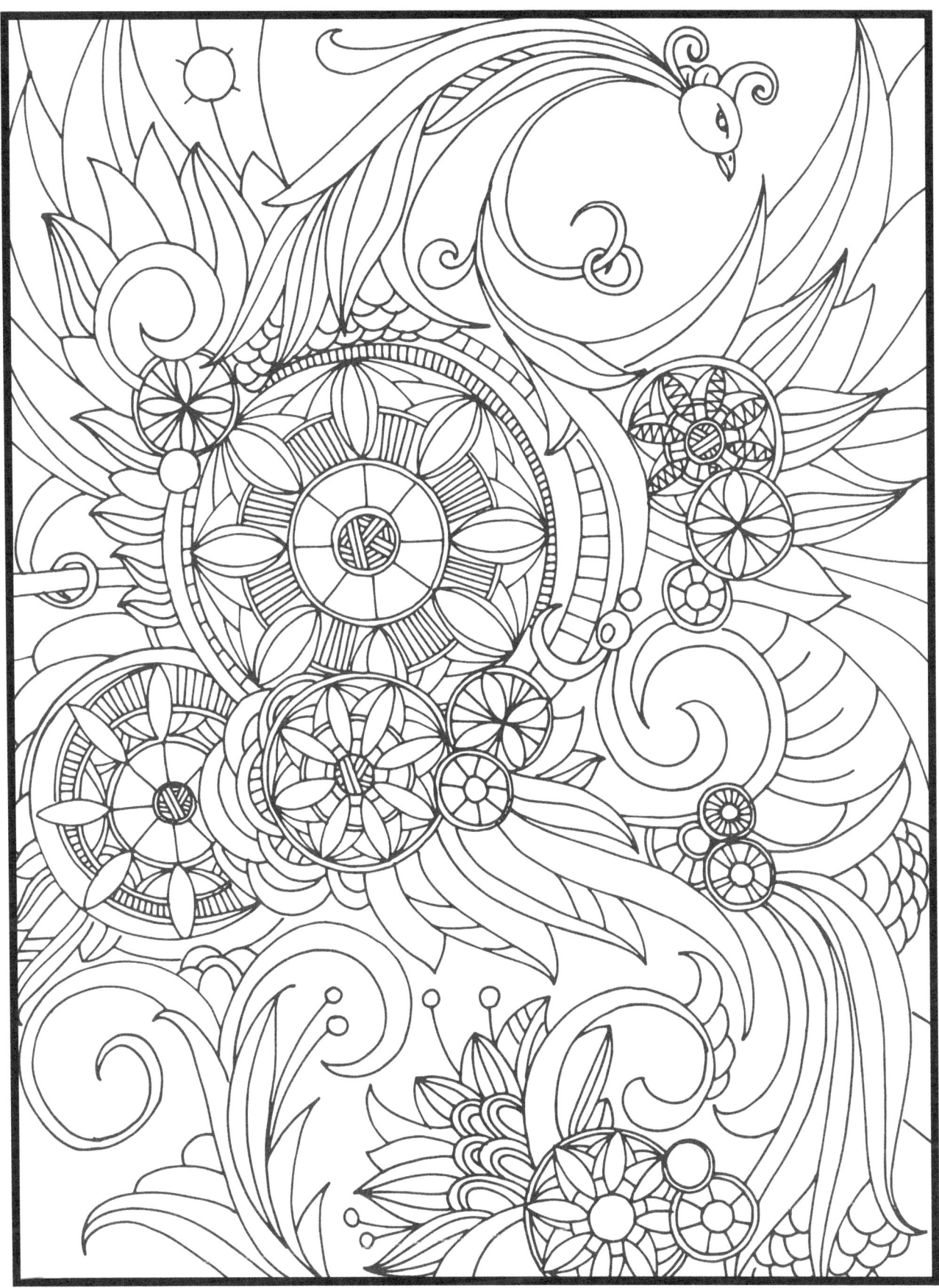

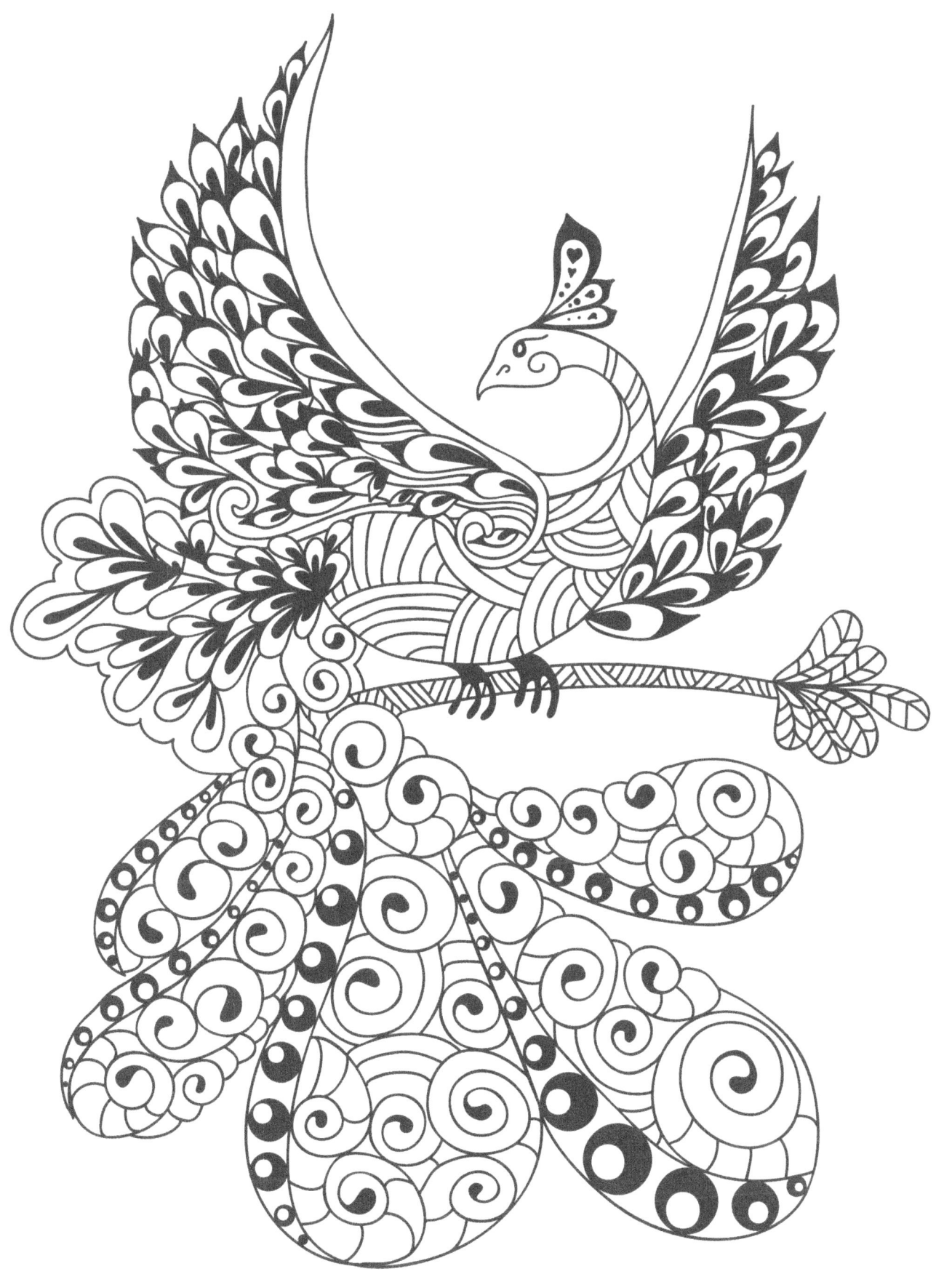

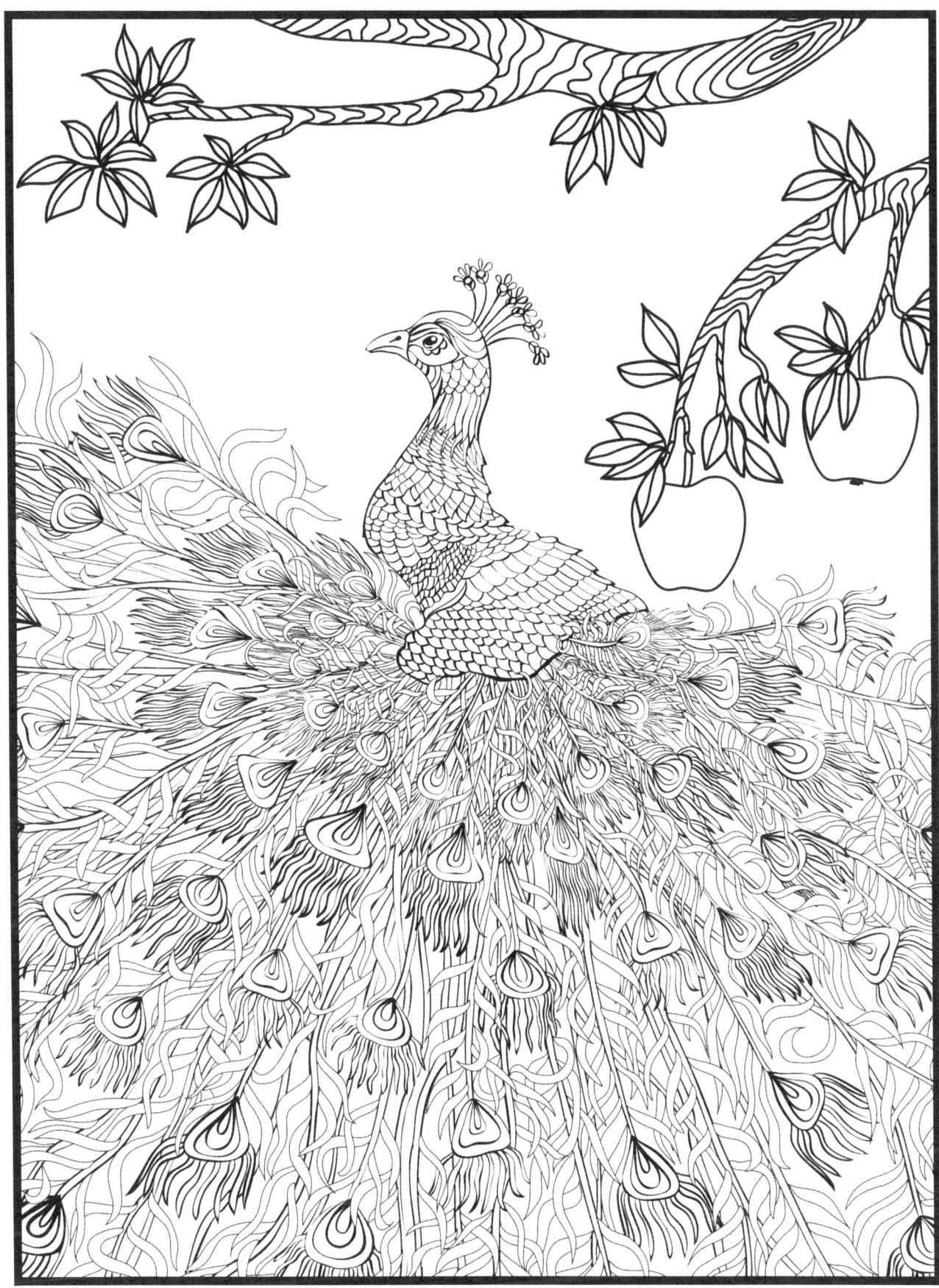

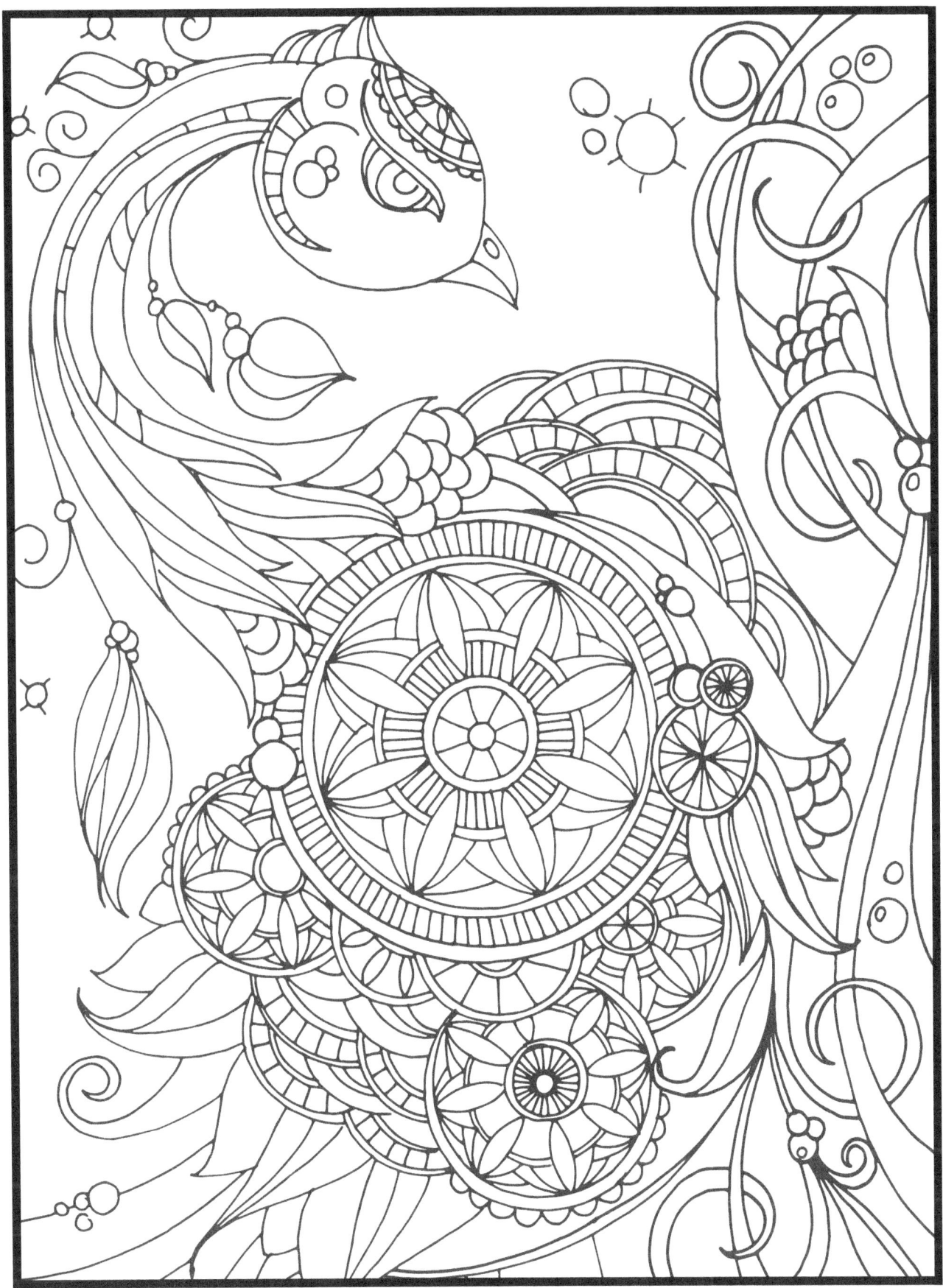

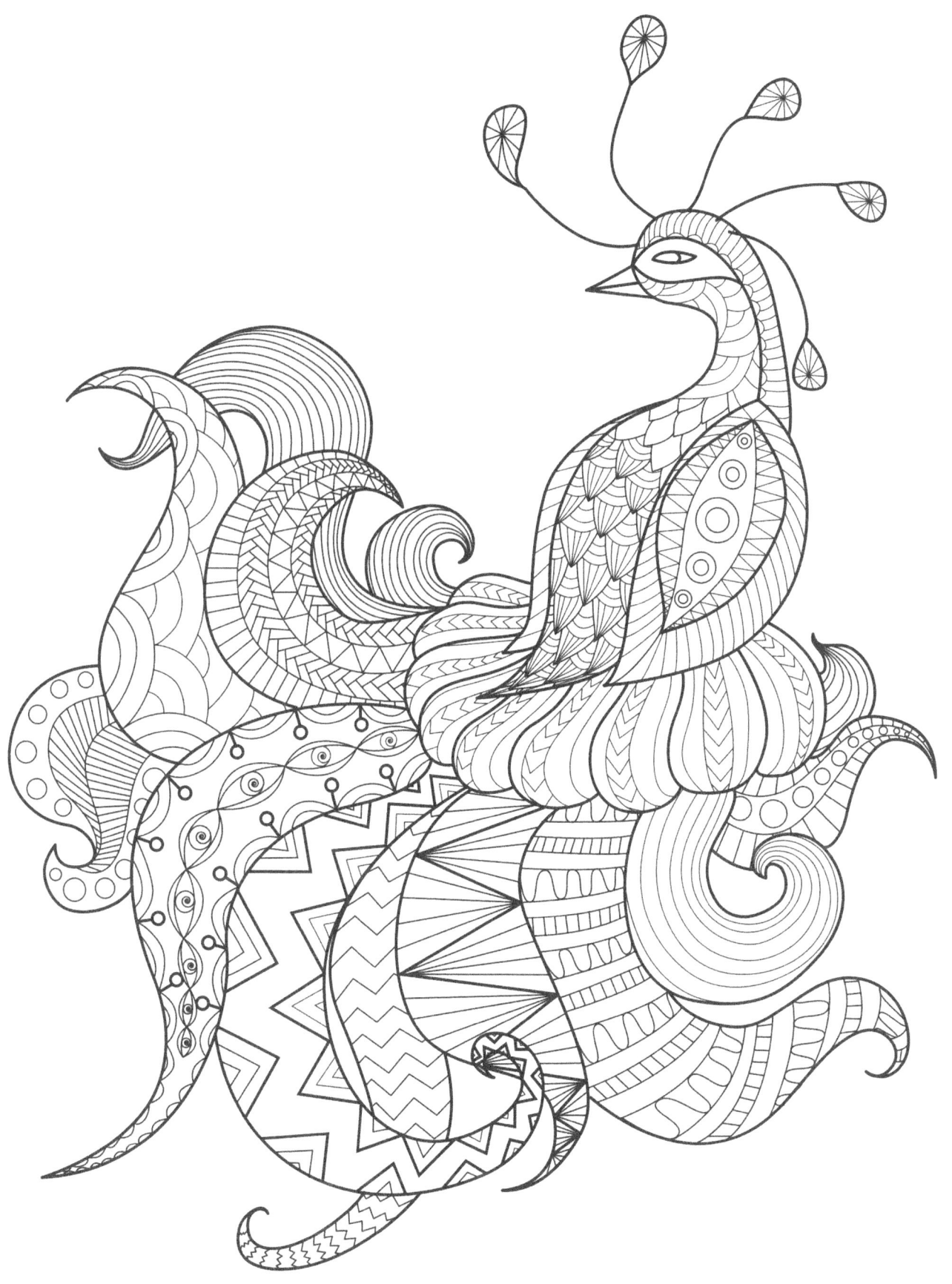

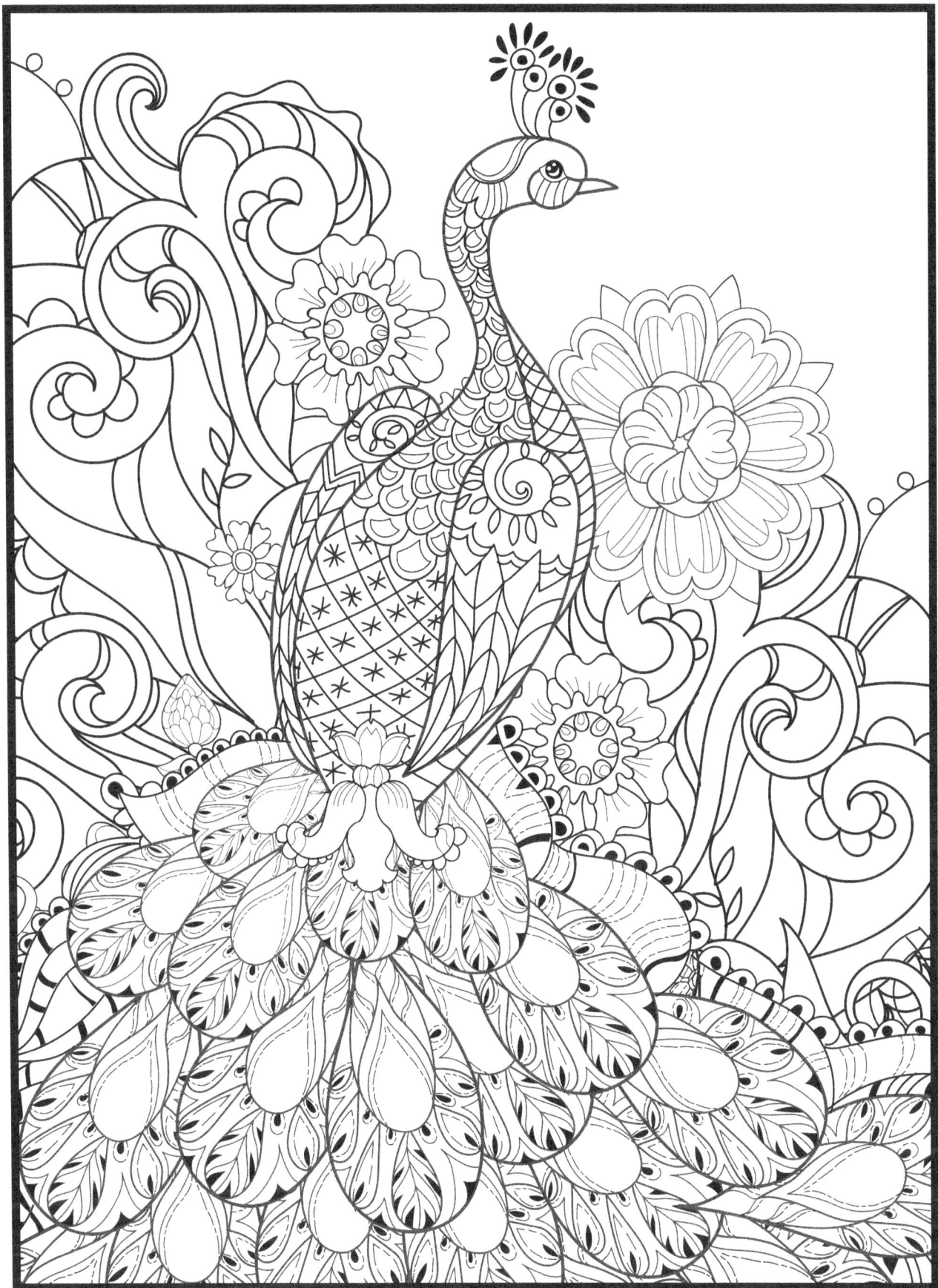

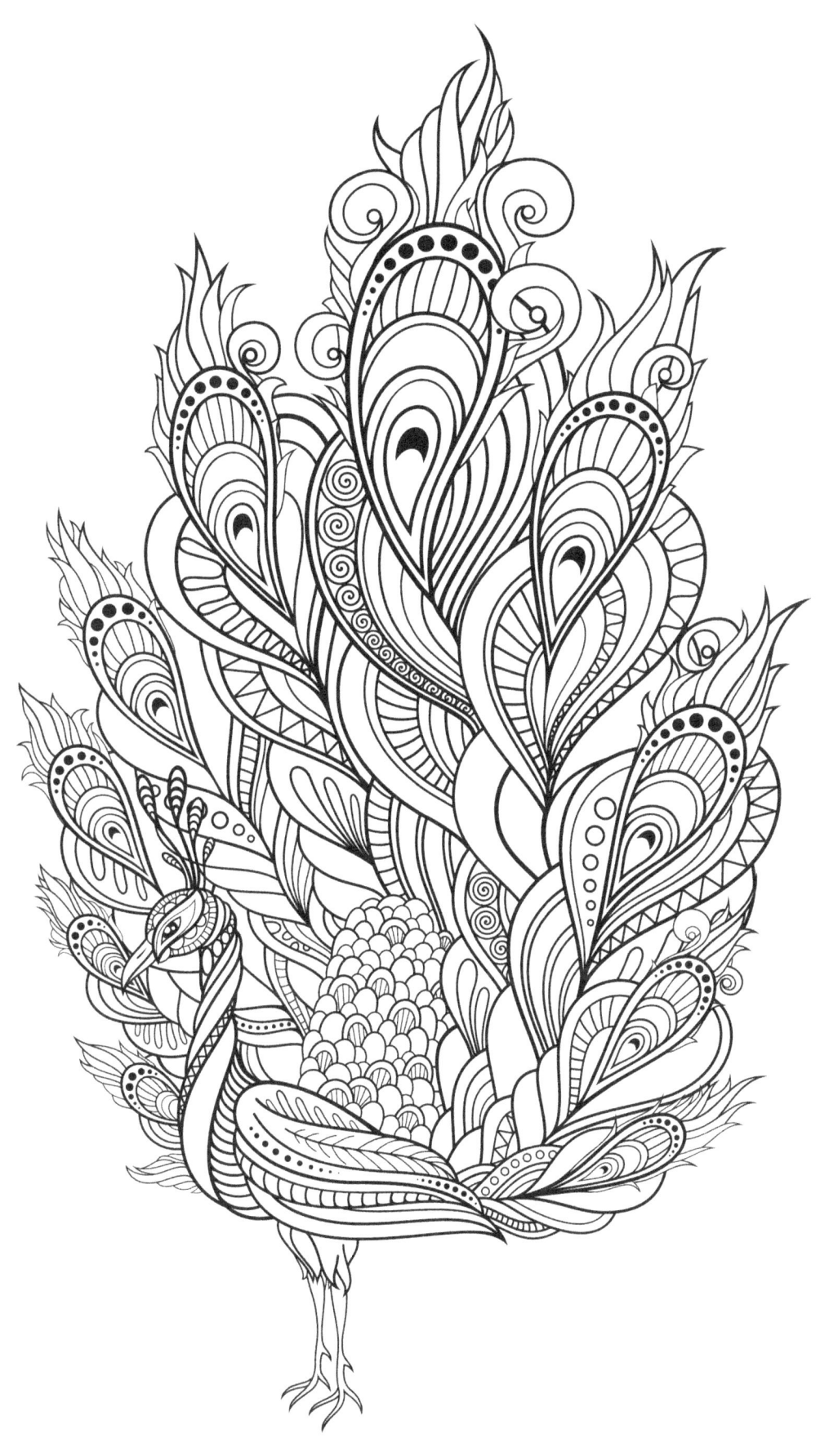

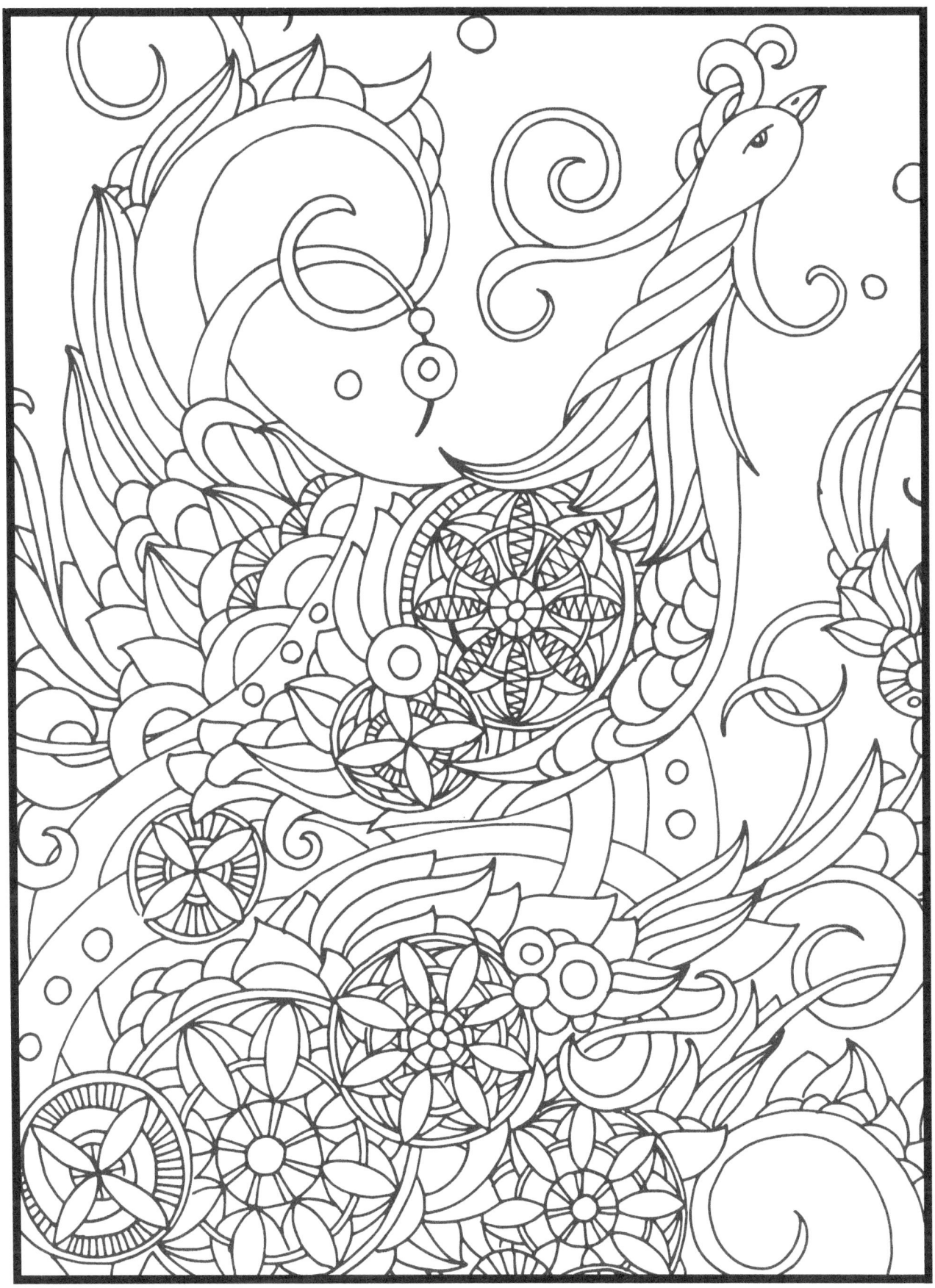

COLOR TEST PAGE

COLOR TEST PAGE